Ready To Retire?

Successful Retirement Planning
To Make
The Best Of The Rest
Of Your Life

Dee Cascio

D1522776

Thank you for selecting Ready To Retire? Successful Retirement Planning To Make The Best Of The Rest Of Your Life.

2014 First edition e-book

2017 Updated and in print

ISBN: 9781521867532

Those who have worked with Dee Cascio say

Attaining life-work balance...
"Through Dee's coaching, I was able to understand that the same set of habits and patterns were creating stumbling blocks in both my work and home life. Dee's gentle guidance supported me in making small, yet significant, changes."

Strength and clarity of purpose during times of transition...
"Dee's excellent coaching helped me clarify my focus. Her skillful nudging kept me on track throughout the transition."

Achieving at maximum personal and professional potential...
"Our sessions have been filled with a mix of focused attention, humor and wisdom from Dee's experience. I highly recommend Dee as a coach!"

Prioritizing goals to make better decisions...
"I worked with Dee to turn my life around. She helped me discover and prioritize objectives towards a new transition."

Successfully navigating a career choice...
"Dee coached me to create a clear vision of success, helped me to develop a personalized, systematic method of attaining my objectives and fostered my self-esteem, which was essential for my sustained change and growth."

Adjusting to retirement...
"After months of trying to 'adjust' to retirement, I asked Dee to be my coach. With her expertise in coaching, Dee provided support to help me discover paths to a new beginning."

"Through coaching, insightful exercises, and reviewing my strengths, I was able to restore my confidence as I reviewed my accomplishments throughout my professional career and my personal life. I now have a retirement lifestyle plan that is working well for me."

Contents

How To Use This Book

Whether you are getting ready to retire or are well into your retirement years, this book will help you get to know yourself and enrich your plan to *make the best of your life for the rest of your life.©* The information in this book is organized so you don't have to read it from cover to cover. Explore the chapters that interest you most or start with those that speak to your current situation.

Planning the perfect retirement is a journey. It's an ongoing quest, not a sprint to the finish line, so take your time with this book. Use it as a guidebook to get from point A—where you are now—to point B—where you want to be in your retirement years.

To get the most from your reading
- Have meaningful conversations about these retirement lifestyle topics with those you love
- Honestly answer the Dig Deeper questions at the end of each chapter
- Find even more retirement information listed on the Resources pages

Chapter 1

There Are Three Things People Seldom Talk About

"There are three things people seldom talk about:

sex, money, and retirement plans."

Tom Haddock

Introduction

Retirement is an old concept with a whole new meaning. Did you know there are approximately seventy-eight million baby boomers born between 1946 and 1964? This means an average of 12,000 people will turn 65 each day until 2029. How many of you fall into that category or within a few years of it? As baby boomers, you will be making a lot of important decisions about your life, and you will also be redefining retirement!

I have heard people say they will probably never retire, and I certainly felt that way. As I entered my mid-fifties, I would even have referred to myself as a Retirement Phobic. I am hoping this book will help you see this stage of life as an exciting adventure to look forward to. By redefining retirement, our generation will have the opportunity to breathe fresh air into an old tradition.

In this book, I will be exploring the lifestyle issues associated with retirement. As a therapist, retirement coach and consultant, I will be asking you a number of questions to explore your own vision for your future and offering suggestions as to how you can survive and thrive in your retirement years.

Unfortunately, too many people think retirement planning is all about money. If you are reading this book, that part of your retirement planning should be mostly behind you. This book is about what you will do with the next twenty-five to thirty-year phase of your life after your 401Ks and IRAs are in place.

My husband, Tom, shared an interesting observation that made me laugh because it is so true. He said there are three things people seldom discuss about their personal lives: sex, money, and their retirement plans. When we talk about sex, it is usually about someone else's behavior and not our own. When we talk about money, it is rare that one discloses their personal financial situation including income and investments. People don't talk about retirement details except when they might retire and where they might live. Retirement is still an abstract notion to many.

This transition is not taboo because it is embarrassing or too personal. It is avoided because it seems too vague to most people. People also are not really sure of all the available possibilities and how to go about navigating this uncharted territory. Most retirement plans contain a lot of buzzwords like *relaxing, traveling, spending time with grandchildren, golf,* etc. Based on what I have learned over the years, this is not a retirement plan destined for success.

I would like you to ponder a few general questions. Can you even imagine being truly retired right now with nothing meaningful to do for the rest of your life? How would you define yourself? What would your retirement vision look like? How many of your friends, colleagues, clients, and peers are struggling with this most important life transition but are not talking about it directly? Have you had retirement conversations with your spouse or partner about your plans, your spouse's plans, and what you would like to plan as a couple?

As a professional retirement counselor and as a trained therapist, I have learned to look at retirement in a new way, and I want the same for you. I am hoping this book will help you see this stage of life as an exciting adventure to look forward to. By redefining retirement, you are the generation that has the opportunity to redefine an old tradition.

My Journey

Ideally, **what you do is not who you are**, but this was not true for me. My career has always been a huge part of who I am, especially because I did not marry until later in life and, although I was a step parent to teenagers, I never had children of my own. Consequently, I have spent most of my adult life on intellectual pursuits. I started my career as a teacher, received my Master's Degree in Counseling and for fifteen years was a high school counselor. In 1986, I received my license as a Professional Counselor and started my private practice. I began my new career by going back to the school system I knew so well to market my private practice. As students and their parents were referred, my practice grew very quickly.

I have always aspired to improving what I could offer clients, so I took several other trainings early in my career. I became trained and certified in hypnosis. An unexpected gift of that experience was that eight of us from that training formed a peer group that met two times a month for over fourteen years. We were fortunate to have had such a great run!

Later, I discovered Imago Relationship Couples Therapy, and I was subsequently trained and certified. The Imago training was also for my own personal relational survival because my husband and I were experiencing the aftershock of the commercial real estate slump in the late 80s through the mid-90s. We had no sooner married before we were hit with these stressors—a new marriage, my new business and financial challenges. Because my husband owned and managed vacation and commercial real estate, this economic situation put a lot of stress on our new marriage. At the same time, managed care was attempting to change the way mental health professionals practice. Believing that Imago Therapy would help us make it through these challenging times, I dragged Tom to an Imago Couples Weekend. I felt drawn to take the training and participating in a couples' weekend with your spouse was a training requirement.

Tom went kicking and screaming and by the end of the weekend we had discovered more about each other and reconnected. We made it through those tough times and learned a lot about each other and our relationship. In fact, we are still learning from and about each other after thirty years. This experience endeared me even more to the value of the work I do as a helping professional, especially with couples, and it also reinforced my identification with work.

This brings me to the most important part of my personal story and how it relates to retirement. We survived this financial ordeal and got back on track with our financial plan for our retirement to be funded by the income from our real estate investments along with my investments.

Tom was ready to talk about the lifestyle part of our retirement plans but I was not at all interested. I was fifty-three and he had just turned sixty at the time. One day, when we were at the beach relaxing and I was reading yet another professional therapy book on couples, he said to me, "Dee, are you reading another therapy book on vacation? Can't you take a break? Look, you know you're not going to want to be a therapist for the rest of your life. At some point you will not want to or have to work anymore. Our real estate investments will support us."

My reptilian brain went right into action and I wanted to strangle him. I responded with irritation. "Are you serious? You were my cheerleader, supporting me as I started my private practice. Now you're talking about retirement! That's not my plan! I love my work and plan to continue doing it for a very long time, maybe forever. My cash flow had gotten us through some tough times." I was like a dog with a bone. You should know in this exchange of words, I threw the book at him—no tissue damage, but I was so angry and clearly not practicing what I preach as a couples therapist. I was just being human and exercising my Italian temper. Well, there was a long silence. Wow—pretty strong! I thought to myself: *what is going on with me?*

Then I thought: *what is going on with him?* Without saying it directly, he was bringing up the topic of retirement, but from my perspective, he could have used another approach. My husband is pretty direct and this approach is not in his nature. Reflecting on this interaction, I think he feared I would not be able to successfully disconnect from my work and be a willing partner in our retirement planning. At that point in time, he was right. Ironically, I had spent the previous several decades of my profession helping clients and couples through a variety of challenging life transitions. But when he wanted to talk about retirement, I was missing in action. Retirement was not in my vocabulary.

The simple truth was that *I was terrified of not working anymore.* It was like standing on the edge of a cliff looking down without a safety net. Every time I was asked on a survey to list my leisure activities, I stumbled and fumbled. After listing my exercise routine, being available to my family and vacationing, there wasn't much left except work. I had to admit that my interests were very limited. If you took my professional identity away, I might just be lost.

After many years of being in my therapy practice, I try to see the significance of events so I can learn from them. I did not totally ignore Tom's comment and we did talk about our reactions after I had settled down. I knew the kinds of retirement lifestyles I had seen in my family and friends' lives weren't what I wanted. I could not see myself in a traditional retirement. These observations affected my attitude towards letting go of work. However, this exercise I was going through begged a bigger question. *If these lifestyles were not what I wanted, what did I want? What could this next stage of my life look like?*

In the middle of my emotional struggle, several significant events happened in our family in a short period of time. Three of my family members were diagnosed with cancer, my sister-in-law was going through a divorce after forty years of marriage, and my dad was diagnosed with Alzheimer's disease and came to live with us. These unexpected events really rocked my world. Suddenly nothing was the same. *Life became more finite.* At a deeper level that fact became more conscious over time.

The fact that life can be shortened in a heartbeat was no longer an intellectual realization but more emotional and my struggles with this life transition began to crystallize. In a few short months, I began to see that there could be more to me than just my work. Fortunately, because of the advancements in medicine and tremendous family support, my family members are all in remission and doing well; my sister-in-law is enjoying single life, and my dad transferred to Assisted Living and referred to this as home until his death two days before his ninety-sixth birthday.

In addition to these life changing events, Tom began modifying some things in his career. He began shifting around some of his real estate investments and doing some business consulting. Usually, when one person in a couple begins to make changes, the other person begins to respond differently.

As I watched both of us making significant changes, I began to see that my resistance was based on fear. When Tom first approached me, I remember thinking to myself, what am I so afraid of? Is my identity so wrapped up in my work that I can't see anything else in my future? Why can't I deal with my almost compulsive need to be working, learning, and improving myself? Ultimately, these concerns came down to one question: what would my life purpose be if I was no longer seeing therapy clients on a daily basis?

In spite of all my initial reluctance, I was becoming more open to conversations with Tom about a semi-retirement lifestyle. We even talked about the possibility of having a second home somewhere in a warmer climate. We began to discuss what would be satisfying for both of us, especially because he was ready to be semi-retired before I was. I began to think about this life transition in stages. Could I have a part-time retirement? I started by reducing my client load and limiting my therapy practice to three days per week.

At this point I had an epiphany. A few years earlier I attended a wedding shower for a fellow therapist who had been in one of the peer groups mentioned earlier. At the shower, I happened to start up a conversation with another guest that I had never met before. She, like me, was a therapist so we began to talk about our individual practices. In this discussion she mentioned she was also a Life Coach and described how she was <u>paralleling</u> her therapy and coaching practices. She explained that in her coaching practice, she was able to work by telephone, giving her a much more flexible work schedule. I was intrigued by this concept, but I never made any further inquiries. In retrospect however, it was clear that a seed had been planted.

Since we were talking more seriously about a semi–retirement lifestyle, I recalled this conversation and began to do some research on coaching. I explored various training programs before discovering Coach University. I took the Life Coach training and subsequently became a Certified Life Coach. One of the most important things that I got out of the training was that it broadened my perspective on the need to achieve more balance in my life. As I completed my training, it dawned on me that most of the people my age were struggling with the same kind of questions about retirement that I was dealing with. As a result, I decided to specialize and make retirement coaching my specific niche. Consequently, I signed up for the training to become certified as a Retirement Coach. Wanting to cover all my bases, I then took the additional training to be certified as a Re-Career Coach. I took these three different trainings for two reasons:

1. To begin a transitional career in coaching while continuing to see a reduced number of clients in my therapy practice.

2. To learn more about retirement and grow into the mind-set of living differently in this stage of life. As I look back on that decision, it's now clear that I became my own first coaching client.

When I started on this journey, one thing was clear to me. I didn't want to be forced into any kind of retirement. I wanted to create a retirement "vacuum" that would gradually draw me in rather than feeling like I was being forced into something. What could easily have been a failed retirement is now on its way to becoming a very successful one. There is no blue print and no road map for this stage of life. Learn all you can so you can make the best choices for you; having discussions with your spouse or partner is essential for a successful transition.

Dig Deeper

When you think of retirement, what lifestyle do you imagine for yourself?

What do you dream of doing in your retirement years that you've never done before?

What might this next stage of your life look like?

Dee Cascio

Chapter 2

Are You Planning To Fail?

"Failing to plan is planning to fail."

Alan Lakein

Create Your Own Legacy And Begin Your Planning Process

My father was a first-generation Italian-American. Both my mother's and father's parents emigrated from Italy and Sicily in the early 1900s to ensure a better life for their families in America. Having had the privilege to grow up in America, my father enlisted in the Air Force during WWII and became a navigator. He was one of many men and women who fought to preserve our freedom and create a legacy that we could all be proud of.

After WWII, my father returned home to New York to continue his life that had been interrupted by the war. My parents, as well as many of yours, were one of many millions of couples who created seventy-eight million American babies. This group of offspring, affectionately called baby boomers, has worked its way through every phase of American life.

Starting in 2011, this generation began turning sixty-five years old in unprecedented numbers. An average of 12,000 Americans will turn sixty-five years old, each and every single day for the next seventeen years. The implication of these massive numbers is overwhelming and there are continuous discussions about this subject on television, radio, and in newspapers and magazines. How will this wave of boomers, soon to be retired, affect medical services, Social Security, and every other part of society?

This information is hardly a surprise because every demographer understood its profound implications by the mid-1960s. In the late 1990s, authors Marc Freedman in his book <u>Prime Time</u> and Ken Dychwalt in his book <u>Age Power</u> wrote about the impending trends of our generation as they aged. They were right! Entire industries have been created to plan financially for this life stage. Over the years, Congress created legislation for 401(k)s, IRAs, Roth IRAs, and numerous other retirement vehicles. For the past half-century, our nation has been overwhelmed with information about the need to plan for retirement so that people won't outlive their money.

Unfortunately, these conversations have concentrated almost exclusively on the financial aspects of retirement. While finances are unquestionably necessary for a comfortable retirement, it is not the only issue. Of equal importance for seventy-eight million Americans is their future **quality of life and happiness**. How will retirees spend their time in the twenty-five to thirty-five or more years after they stop working? Our ancestors fought for our freedom so that our generation could create a lifestyle that would ultimately enable us to plan for a fulfilling Retirement Career. Let's honor their sacrifices by beginning with the planning process and create a legacy that we can all be proud of.

Let's Talk About The Importance Of Planning

You've all heard the phrase *"Failing to plan is planning to fail."* I'd like to give you a metaphor that might help put planning into perspective. Suppose you had good friends or family members who always talked about their lifelong dream of going to Italy for a month. After listening to their dream for years, one day they excitedly tell you they have finally decided to go the following month and they've already made their plane reservations. They've saved for a long time so money isn't an issue.

While you're excited for them, you're also amazed when you realize that the only planning they've actually done is the purchase of the plane tickets and travelers checks. Where would they stay, what would they do? Your friends sense from the kinds of questions you're asking that you have some apprehension about their vacation plans. They brush off your concerns by saying reservations aren't a problem and they'll book their tours, hotels, museums, etc. once they have arrived in Europe. They want to get the "lay of the land" before they make any definite plans. You wonder how their dream will be realized since they're going in August, which is the busiest month of the year. What if they can only find substandard hotel accommodations or if there are only a few available tours that have not been sold out? Suppose the tours that are available are not to the places they have always dreamed of seeing?

Unfortunately, leaving things like a vacation to chance can result in a huge disappointment and leave one with a very incomplete feeling. Failing to plan one's retirement lifestyle will have much more devastating consequences than going to Europe without reservations. The irony of this hypothetical situation is that many people actually spend more time planning their vacations than they spend planning their retirement lifestyle.

Optimally, you should begin planning at least three to five years before you retire. Just as many of us have used the guidance of a financial planner, seeking the support of a Lifestyle Retirement Coach to help you plan your dream retirement can be very helpful. Third-party assistance will usually help you avoid mistakes that could be costly both financially and emotionally.

In another scenario, consider the couple who moves away from family and friends without thinking about how their move will affect their lives. After they discover how much they miss their loved ones, they see no alternative but to move back. This happens much more frequently than you might think.

Planning has nothing to do with how intelligent, educated, creative, or resourceful you are. It's about realizing just how complicated this transition can be. Retirement can be like a complex mechanical machine with many moving parts whose function is not always obvious. It's unmistakably the only transition in life that has no clear definition of what will happen next except that one day you'll wake up in the morning with no job to go to. You may leave work voluntarily or involuntarily, but make no mistake about it; you will eventually leave your job.

Planning For A Successful Retirement The Failsafe Way

I have also experienced "failure to plan for retirement" in my personal life. Like many others considering retirement, I have traveled the maze of this transition by having numerous conversations with my husband, friends, and family who have also made this change. My husband and I have shared our excitement, expectations, and fears as we realized just how complicated this maze can be. It became clear that there were many decisions to make and people to consider other than ourselves.

In the process, we had to locate resources, identify and deal with our emotions, and fight the pervasive temptation to do nothing out of fear of making a mistake. Fear of failure and fear of making a mistake are my personal challenges even though I have made great strides in this area. Fortunately, Tom is more comfortable with taking risks so he brings balance to that part of our marriage.

Bringing Clarity To This Transition

I know myself well enough to realize the best way to address my fears is to educate myself. For example, in 1995, my husband began to subscribe to a magazine entitled *Where To Retire*. As I began "to get into it," I started to read his old copies of this magazine. The articles in this magazine talked about places to retire, but more important to me, the magazine featured articles that described important new concepts in retirement living.

The articles focused on lifestyle trends, taxes in various geographical areas, cost comparisons, average weather temperatures, crime levels, cultural amenities, and higher education opportunities just to name a few. Some of the lifestyles they featured include retiring to college towns, beach towns, the mountains, small towns, large cities, low cost locations, and rural settings. Other articles focused on people who stay in their original home but traveled to a second home during the winter months like my husband and I have chosen to do. Still other retirees remained in their current home and just travel more frequently. Because we are all so unique, each of our visions will be different. Each of you has the potential to make retirement anything you want it to be. However, regardless of what path you eventually choose to take, planning is a must.

We have found that gathering information years before this important transition has worked well for us. I highly recommend collecting a personal library of as much information as you can get your hands on. There are many books, magazines, and newspaper articles available that can help you get started. Simply start a file called retirement and put everything you can find about retirement into that file. Use this information to begin thinking about the kind of lifestyle you want and how your desires can complement your partner's dreams.

Talk to those who have retired and learn from their experiences, good or bad. Communicating with your spouse and family about what you are learning and the kinds of ideas your research reveals are important aspects of effective planning. Information and educated decisions build the foundation of a successful transition.

These focused and honest discussions helped my husband and me share our needs, values, interests, desires, and concerns. Eventually, we were able to make decisions that worked well for both of us. For example, our research and numerous discussions resulted in our selecting an urban lifestyle in Tampa, Florida, for our second home location. After seven years, the wisdom of that decision has been confirmed. Tampa is only two hours by plane from our home in Virginia so we're able to go there once a month. Our schedule includes working the first three weeks of each month in Virginia and spending the last ten days in Tampa. Our second home is on the water but only a short walk to a variety of interesting activities. Like most of Florida, especially the Gulf Coast, Tampa has a relatively warm climate during the winter months and offers abundant social, environmental, and intellectual stimulation. We love the contrast to our more conventional lifestyle in Virginia.

Taking Action

The book entitled <u>Repacking Your Bags: Lighten Your Load For The Rest Of Your Life</u> by Richard Leider and David Shapiro talks about doing the research necessary if your retirement plans include relocation. Lieder and Shapiro recommend:

- Be prepared if you are planning to work or re-career. Find out if there is a market for what you do now or what you plan to do if you are re-careering in a new location.
- Write to the local Chamber of Commerce for information on the area. Find out if the area has what you are looking for in the way of educational facilities, restaurants, culture, healthcare, etc.
- Subscribe to the local newspaper and learn what is going on in the new location. Take a weekend getaway to the retirement destination you are considering first and experience the flavor of the environment. Eat at local restaurants, take walks, and educate yourself by asking residents about their experiences there. Then take a longer visit to get a true feel for actually living there. Remember, however, that the essentials for a successful retirement are not the same as what is needed for a successful vacation.
- Read books written about the town, city, or state so you can make the best educated decision for you.

In addition, ask yourself the Dig Deeper questions at the end of this chapter about where you are considering living in retirement. Discuss these suggestions and questions with your spouse or partner, or if you are single, with family and friends before you begin your retirement planning process.

Failed Retirements

In retirement, there is no "one size fits all." What many want and ultimately choose is very personal to each individual. Even within a marriage, your spouse will have expectations that are different from yours. Regardless of the countless variations in lifestyles, it is how you navigate these differences that will determine how happy and successful you are in your retirement. Even if only one spouse is bored, unfulfilled, lost, unhappy, or has regrets about retiring, the effects of this will be felt by both and will be a recipe for a failed retirement.

Conditions For A Failed Retirement

Consider some of the following myths and the truth about them.

Myth 1 *I will be able to figure it out on my own after I retire.*

In other words, wing it. Some of us believe we can figure it out as we go but the reality is that we will have twenty-five to thirty more years in retirement than our ancestors did. It is easy for many of us to fall into idle busyness and then wonder why we are bored and restless. This stage of life is the only one for which there is no blueprint like all of the other stages of your life, so it may require that you enlist more resources for support. This stage requires:

- Reading books about retirement
- Having conversations with significant people in your life
- Exploring where to live and how to live
- Strategizing about retiring at the right time to the right place
- Deciding whether or not to stay in place
- Finding purpose and meaning in your life
- Deciding if you will work, volunteer, or start a new career in this life stage
- Developing self-knowledge and understanding of all aspects of yourself

What will you do with no schedule, no family, and no friends close by? How will you deal with the loss of medical professionals you have relied on for so many years? These are very critical decisions that should not be postponed until after the fact.

Myth 2 *I'll make it easy and just follow the crowd.*

Instead of exploring what it is they need in order to define their ideal retirement, these people default to someone else's plan. There are so many different interests, needs, activity levels, and connections to family/friends for each of us that following the crowd may leave a person disillusioned and unfulfilled. Why is this? Some are so used to others leading that they also follow this pattern in retirement planning. Still, others have no idea how to plan because "they do not know what they do not know."

At one of my presentations, a participant said that he and his wife, along with four other couples, had been discussing retiring to the same place as a group. This had all of the elements of a failed retirement because none of them had done any planning other than to discuss where they might live. Friendships are important but this group had let that element of their lives define how, when, and where they would retire. It is hard enough to reach agreement for each couple let alone multiple couples. The participant acknowledged that after several years, this group had not been able to make any decisions.

Myth 3 *My spouse and I will be happy to be spending more time together.*

Often this stage of life throws two people together who have had little day-to-day involvement during the working phase of their lives. Suddenly they are together every day. In some cases, one has been home and the other, typically the husband, has been at work eight to ten hours a day. After retirement, a couple may be home every day with no idea as to how they will spend this time together. One spouse may feel responsible for creating the schedule when previously he or she has been free to make their own plans. As a result, conflict may arise. It is so important that a couple communicate well in advance of either or both retiring.

Tom and I had many discussions long before we became more serious about our plans and long before I was ready for these discussions. At times, it was challenging for me. However, I am forever grateful to him. Our discussions helped me to realize how unprepared I was for this transition. I came to realize how much preparation I needed to make for this life stage. I had to do my homework before I could actually begin planning. By the third year of my definition of part-time-retirement, I really began enjoying it.

There are many people retiring who have not done the introspective work to clarify what they need in this new phase of life. A person's direction in retirement should be from the inside out, not from the outside in. Maintaining some level of autonomy, individually and as a couple, in making these important decisions is imperative to insure that you will be living your own lifestyle and not someone else's.

Myth 4 *I will make the decision on when to* retire.

How can you pace your transition to meet your own needs and your spouse's? Some careers allow people to retire gradually over time by reducing their schedule one day at a time over a period of months. This is called a *phased retirement*. Others have a specific age that they have to retire. For decades, airline pilots were forced to retire at age sixty. This was devastating for so many of them because they were still healthy and able to perform their jobs well.

Fortunately for airline pilots today, the age limit has been extended to a more realistic age of sixty-five because many pilots are still in excellent health and are able to safely continue flying planes. Some law and accounting firms require their partners to retire at a certain age to make room for younger partners. For many firms, there is no transition time but there is an opportunity to anticipate this transition and plan for it.

Fortunately, my psychotherapy profession allows me to phase out gradually so I can pursue other endeavors like retirement coaching, volunteer work, new activities, and travel. Do you have a career that allows you to phase out gradually or one that has a mandatory retirement age? Could you be caught off guard by your company downsizing and offering you an early retirement? Will you be ready?

Myth 5 *All I need to be happy in my retirement is a good financial plan.*

I've intentionally left the biggest myth to the very end. Unfortunately, this is the most significant set-up for disaster. There are two issues involved here. *Quantity* and *quality*. People think the only action they need to take is to plan to have enough money—quantity. While this is certainly a very important part of the plan, it is only part of the process. Creating a successful lifestyle — quality—is just as important. It is unsettling to realize some people spend more time planning mundane aspects of their lives than they spend on the lifestyle decisions that will impact the next twenty-five to thirty years of their lives. Don't be the one who makes this mistake. Make sure you do the important work for retirement lifestyle planning so you can design the best retirement for you.

Conditions For A Successful Retirement

How can you avoid mistakes that could lead to a failed retirement? The above issues and many more are important factors to consider in planning for a successful transition. Retirement should be like a designer suit which is customized specifically for you. It should not be like a suit you buy off the rack at a department store.

Please consider the following suggestions:

- Explore professional support and expertise available in designing a successful retirement. Don't try to wing it.
- Have discussions with your spouse or partner early and often in your planning.
- Refrain from following the crowd and individualize your plans to reflect who you are and what you need.
- Anticipate this transition by planning for it. Embrace this exciting new phase of your life by considering all of the options ahead of time.
- Explore a phase-out plan within your career area if at all possible. Be thinking now about other career possibilities if you want to include work in your next life chapter.
- Do an attitude check. How you really feel about retirement will affect your motivation to explore new ideas and plan for success.

Dig Deeper

Where will you get professional support and expertise for planning your retirement?

Where do you want to live in your retirement years?

- Is this really where you want to be?
- Will you be able to thrive, be stimulated, and maintain current interests there?
- Will you be able to relax there when you want to?
- Will you be able to do the level of physical activity there that you believe is necessary for a healthy retirement?
- Will you be able to get back to family and friends quickly in case of an emergency or just to visit?

Are you clearly communicating your desires to your partner and family?

What is your career phase-out plan?

How will you repurpose your experience, skills and talents in your retirement career?

How will you replace the benefits work currently provides? (more on this in Chapter 9)

Retirement Resources

Books
Repacking Your Bags: Lighten Your Load For The Rest Of Your Life by Richard Leider and David Shapiro

Web Sites
Retirement Options
http://www.retirementoptions.com/Retirement_Coach_Directory.asp?state=VA

Dee Cascio

Chapter 3

Learn From My Mistakes

"It is necessary for us to learn from others' mistakes.

You will not live long enough to make them all yourself."

Hyman Rickover

What I Learned From This Life Experience

I want to share what I learned over this five to six-year process of preparing for retirement and helping others. Most notably:

- Sometimes our spouses and friends encourage us to stretch into places we are afraid to go. Looking back, I realized that I needed to make that stretch.
- Communicating with your spouse or partner about what you both want and making it happen is paramount to a successful life stage transition.
- Singles need to have friends and family as a sounding board for their plans.

Mike And Mary—A Story Of Communication And Resolution

I met Mike while working on a committee through a local coaching organization. When he learned I was a therapist as well as a retirement coach, he began to tell me his story. He had been working at a large company as an internal coach while he built his private coaching practice. His wife, who had retired two years earlier from a local school system, wanted to buy a condo at the beach. As they talked, they realized they disagreed on where they wanted to live in retirement. He felt she did not understand that he still wanted and needed to work and be closer to the action. She had her heart set on a place at the beach where she could truly relax. They had reached an impasse in their communication and relationship. I could hear fear and concern in his voice.

The fear was that he knew they couldn't afford two houses and he didn't know what would happen if they couldn't resolve it.

After our discussion, I found out that an Imago Couples' therapist I know, who is also a Relationship Coach, was doing a demonstration at a coaching conference and needed a couple for a demonstration. The workshop was designed to show how coaching could be used to help couples who didn't need therapy but would benefit from coaching support. I asked Mike and his wife to volunteer to bring their issue to the demo. He was able to convince her that this might be good for both of them and she came willingly.

It might sound too dramatic if I told you they had a major breakthrough but that's exactly what happened. When they were both better able to hear each other's needs with the assistance of a coach, they were able to gain insight, understanding, empathy, and found a progressive solution. The fact that Mike and Mary had therapy in the past helped. After the session and more discussions, they sold their much larger, expensive home and bought a smaller home in a less expensive 55+ community. With equity from their home sale and a smaller monthly expense for their new home, they had options they didn't have before and were closer to realizing their dream. This breakthrough may not have happened if they had not had some assistance talking about their differences and developing a mutual plan. Their story truly speaks to the power and importance of communicating with your partner early in the planning stages. They are now closer to purchasing their second home.

Some Other Lessons I Learned From My Training And Life Experience

- Retirement needs to be considered as a transition to a new career with a brand new definition of work activities.
- If we plan well, retirement will be very different from our parents' retirement.
- While you are moving away from your current career, do you have some idea of what you are moving towards? It is extremely important to identify this early on, even if you change your mind. Start somewhere.
- Retirement is very personal and different for each of us depending on our individual preferences and circumstances so be careful to not follow the crowd.
- What works for another couple may not work for you.
- Planning your retirement lifestyle is just as important as financial planning. You can have enough money for a great retirement but how you spend your time will determine the actual success of this phase of life.
- Life can be shortened without notice so plan enough time to enjoy the fruits of your lifelong efforts.
- A successful retirement is when a person is truly happy, feels purposeful, is fulfilled, and is having fun in life.

My Lifestyle Today

Today, I work part-time in my psychotherapy practice for the first two days of the week. Over the next two years, I plan to phase out of my private psychotherapy practice. I really have enjoyed my thirty years as a therapist, but being in my office four to five days a week seeing clients would interfere with the future retirement plans that Tom and I had discussed. Coaching, consulting, and doing presentations gives me more flexibility in my schedule. I use the rest of the week to build my Retirement Lifestyle Coaching and Consulting practice.

In addition to my therapy and coaching practice, I belong to Toastmasters, an organization dedicated to developing public speaking. To further enhance my public speaking skills, I joined the National Speakers Association. These two organizations have really helped me to confront my fear of public speaking. I'm sure that many of you can relate to having this fear hold you back in your life. I didn't want to experience that fear anymore. I enjoy the camaraderie with peers while learning new skills, which I believe are essential to my encore career. Having this experience has helped me to realize that I want my retirement presentations to reach larger audiences. When people express their ideas, concerns, and challenges along with their dreams in a group, there is much more learning going on.

A unique feature of coaching is that many coaches work the first three weeks of the month and take the fourth week off. They use this last week to develop other aspects of their businesses, work on passive income projects, do presentations to groups, and travel. I have adopted this schedule in both my private therapy practice and my coaching practice. I have been taking off the last ten days of each month since June of 2007. To take advantage of this extra non-work time, we usually go to our condo in Tampa, Florida where I do the following kinds of things.

- I do some work there but I also spend time relaxing, read, ride on Tom's Vespa with him, visit museums, attend plays, entertain visitors, and go to the beach.
- I joined the Rotary Club of Herndon. I liked it so much that I attend some Rotary meetings in Tampa where I meet new people and add to my social network.
- I joined the Tampa Bay Coaching Association where I have met many like-minded professionals and have developed joint projects with some of them.
- I write monthly newsletters and presentation outlines for my coaching practice, reviving a skill I have not exercised during my years in private practice.

All these activities are a part of an incredible learning curve which I believe is necessary to explore this new and exciting stage of life. Learning new skills associated with these activities is my way of bringing purpose and meaning into my life while helping others do the same. Questions to ask yourself:

- What is it you have always wanted to do but never had the time, opportunity, or the courage to do?
- What are you passionate about that will give you joy and satisfaction?
- How will you give back some of what you have been given?

Never Say Never

Our grandson David became a member of our family at five years of age when my step-son married David's mother, who had moved here from Columbia, South America. When David first arrived, his whole world was alien; a new language, a new country, a new school, and a whole new family. It was obviously overwhelming to this little guy. Seeing him initially struggle, my husband decided to make his assimilation into the United States a priority. Tom wanted him to grow up feeling secure with his new country and family. This meant giving him positive male role models. Tom decided to create a tradition of the guys' afternoon out.

Tom made a point of spending at least one afternoon a week with David, going out to eat or to the movies, exploring the zoo, or sometimes just taking a walk. I think it's an understatement to say the two of them bonded in a very special way and shared some wonderful conversations over the years. David would occasionally spend weekends with both of us.

I will never forget a conversation that I witnessed. It was when David turned eleven and Tom began talking to him about the process of growing up and becoming a man. David was complaining about the girls in his classroom. In a lighthearted moment, Tom playfully told David that someday he was going to like girls. David quickly retorted, "That's not going to happen!" Over the next several years, it was fun watching the two of them teasing each other about liking girls. Tom: "Someday you're going to like girls!" David: "You're wrong because I'm _never_ going to like girls!" Fast forward seven years— do I really have to tell you what he thinks of girls these days?

Watching this cute drama unfold between the two of them reminds me of frequent conversations I have had over the years with friends, relatives, and acquaintances. Some have been as adamant as David by proclaiming "_I will never retire._" This refusal to even consider the possibility of any lifestyle beyond the present work-a-day world is not foreign to me. Before finding my own rewarding retirement lifestyle path, I felt exactly the same way.

But let's face it: just like most teenage boys eventually discover girls, most of you will eventually change or leave your work situation. Sometimes it's by choice, other times it's a result of external factors such as a layoff, health issue, etc. Whatever the circumstances, if you look openly and creatively at retirement for the variety of opportunities it presents, you can find a new, very rewarding lifestyle.

Unfortunately, too many people dig in their heels and put off retirement for as long as possible. They commit to that "over my dead body" and "never!" mind-set. Unfortunately, this resistance only prolongs the inevitable and makes moving forward in life with a positive attitude difficult. They become stuck, missing some wonderful life adventures.

So, Why Do People Refuse To Retire?

People continue working past the time when they might otherwise retire for various reasons.

Unfortunately, some are compelled to work because of economic circumstances. We all know people who have encountered adverse conditions or haven't planned effectively for their financial needs. Others are fortunate enough not to encounter financial difficulty but continue to work because they honestly don't know what else to do with their time. Their entire life, as well as their identity, is so tied up in their work they don't see anything else. I immediately recognize them because I was a member in good standing in that club for many years. Finally, there are those who truly love what they do and want to work a few more years before they phase out.

For those who need to work for financial reasons, do the homework necessary to explore employment in a new career that reflects your values and allows you some time to enjoy retirement. It's unlikely you will make as much money as you currently do, but with lifestyle changes you might feel more secure financially.

A new concept practiced by some boomers is to begin experimenting with retirement while you're still working. It's called, "practicing retirement." This trend involves adding a new hobby or volunteer interests that you can do even before you retire. It is one of the ways of discovering aspects about yourself that you didn't even know were there.

For those who continue to work because it is the only way they can identify themselves as productive and satisfied, they can begin creating more balance in their life by discovering other aspects of themselves. They need to stretch into pursuing a variety of other interests. You don't need to lose your sense of self as you transition to your desired retirement lifestyle. Always remember that as rewarding as your work may be or as prestigious as your work title is, it is not the essence of who you are. Your strengths and talents led you to your career and achievements. In the same way, they can lead you to another quality lifestyle after traditional full-time work.

It's important to find a healthy balance between work and other interests. This balance is important in all life stages.

Nothing says a retired person's life shouldn't include work as an important part of a balanced lifestyle. After all, work isn't the enemy of a successful retirement but an attitude of rigidity, inflexibility, and resistance is. Whether we **choose** to work or **need** to work as part of our retirement, the form of work and the balance achieved with our other life interests is key to establishing a rewarding next stage in life. Remember, there is life after work as well as work after retirement. You get to choose.

Embracing Life's Transitions

Retirement is just another one of life's many transitions. Most of my contemporaries have progressed somewhat effortlessly through life's earlier transitions. They left home at eighteen years old, went to college, and graduated. They then found their first job, got married, had children, and settled into a career. However, in spite of our generation's earlier success with making these often difficult life transitions look easy, the idea of retirement has left many confused, anxious, and fearful.

It's interesting to contrast our generation's experience with transitions to those that are going on in our children and grandchildren's generation. After college most of us struck out on our own by getting our own apartment. That's almost unheard of today as a large percentage of college graduates move back into their old bedroom for long periods of time. There is an increasing number of twenty-five to thirty-five year olds still needing financial support from their parents. Obviously, the high rate of unemployment is one of the factors. The "40 Year Old

Virgin" and "Failure to Launch" are two contemporary movies illustrating this younger generation's inability to successfully move to the next stage of life. Our generation, on the other hand, made these transitions effortlessly. Now it's time to be successful at doing it once again. What's holding you back?

Jump!

News anchor Charles Gibson was interviewed about his retirement and relayed his initial resistance to it as feeling as though he was "jumping off a cliff." He went on to say he later realized that in his lifetime, he had jumped several times before. At each of life's transitions, we "jump" in a sense—to a new marriage, to having children, to living in another place, to a new job. At the time, each transition can feel daunting, but you know that you must keep moving forward to experience, grow, and live. Gibson further said that once he moved from his initial dread of what he was leaving and focused on what was to come, his resistance changed to anticipation of great things.

I encourage you to begin this new season of your life with a new mind-set. Consider retirement not as an ending but as a new beginning with many opportunities to discover more about yourself than you ever knew was possible.

Are You Retirement Phobic?

A retirement phobic is someone who is reluctant to explore the next vital stage of their life. Their reluctance is not necessarily because they love their job, but because they are terrified of what life will look like without work to provide their identity. You may not think of people you know as retirement phobic, but I would imagine you know several because many of us do. People have said to me, "I will never retire" and express their reasons that always sound legitimate. However, underneath I observe something different. As a recovering "retirement phobic" myself, I can relate to their feelings and am familiar with all of their talking points.

Answering The Question

You need to be honest with yourself and try to determine what you are really afraid of. Do you find yourself avoiding this important life transition? Do you feel like you are on the edge of a cliff like Charlie Gibson, or are you holding on to your current work out of fear, with no plan or retirement vision? If these general comments resonate with you, please consider asking yourself the compelling questions in the Dig Deeper section.

Dig Deeper

What are you passionate about that will give you joy and satisfaction?

What would stop you from retiring tomorrow if money wasn't an issue?

How can you define retirement as the next stage of your life's career?

What are your fears about retirement and how will you face these fears?

How can you move through your fear and embrace your life's passions?

After retirement, can you imagine beginning a new career?

What skills have you used in other transitions that you can use in your retirement transition?

How would you rate your present life satisfaction and your anticipated life satisfaction?

How do you define yourself separate from work?

What are your interests and if you have few, how could you change that?

How would you spend your time if you didn't work as much as you do?

What contributions do you make to your community?

What are you passionate about that could turn into a part-time occupation?

Is your significant relationship strong enough to sustain a collaborative retirement lifestyle?

Retirement Resources

Magazines

Where to Retire

Web Sites
Special coaching needs of retirees
http://www.retirementlifestylestrategies.com/retirees.html

Your coaching options
http://www.retirementlifestylestrategies.com/retirement-coaching-programs.html

Values Inventory

http://www.whatsnext.com

Chapter 4

Nothing Ever Stays The Same

"Be who you are and say what you feel, because those who mind don't matter and those who matter don't mind."

Dr. Seuss

How Well Do You Cope With Change?

Last fall while I was sitting in our sun room watching the leaves fall, I was aware of another change in seasons. I regretted the loss of the long, lazy days of summer but still looked forward to the crisp and colorful days of autumn. This change in seasons always reminds me of how many adjustments we all experience throughout our lives.

In spite of its excitement, all change carries with it the risk of the unknown and the unexpected. Some find these transitions exciting and welcome the challenge. They are able to go with the flow. Others follow the path of change reluctantly, dragging their heels all the way and feeling threatened. Perhaps their anxiety is caused by their fear that they won't be able to navigate the risk involved and the ultimate transition.

Many of us have anxieties that create barriers to change, especially as we age. In an effort to cope with this phenomenon, you may hear these kinds of comments: I am too old to learn new technology; this approach works, why modify it; I am too busy, too disorganized, too overwhelmed, too set in my ways. Does this sound familiar? Do any of us really want to end up thinking this way?

It is easy to justify whatever we put our minds to. Opportunities abound when we choose the path of change and growth. This change can open up a whole new world to us. Research shows that our brains are perfectly capable of learning new behaviors at any age. It is only our attitudes and beliefs that stand in the way.

Changes And Transitions In Retirement

As you transition to retirement, your ability to deal with change becomes even more important and necessary. Your career will change either because you have to or want to retire or because you have decided to try something different. Once you have made this change, you may decide you want to work part time, volunteer, or do something else you have always wanted to do. Other things will be impacted by this decision.

You may be wondering what the difference is between change and transition. Change represents a physical move to a different place or a different position or anything that is no longer the way it used to be. You can see it because it is tangible, concrete, and visible. A transition, on the other hand, is the emotional and psychological adjustment to this physical change. It is invisible and intangible.

Socially, your friends will change as you transition from work. You will keep some friendships and lose others. As you begin a new life, you will meet new friends, discover new environments, and experience a different commute each day as you navigate different life adjustments. You may learn new skills and rediscover skills that you have not used in a long time.

As we age, we will also experience new challenges to our health. You may discover elevated cholesterol, high blood pressure, or pain in certain parts of your body. Fortunately, you will reap the benefits of progressive medical research as new ways continue to evolve to treat these chronic ailments. You may also decide to change your routine and include daily exercise and develop a healthier lifestyle. Why not make these changes? Doing this may help you age well and could even extend your life.

You and your spouse/partner may decide to buy a second home that you travel to during the winter months. Moving back and forth between two homes requires a degree of flexibility that represents the ultimate willingness to cope with change. However, you may decide to move out of your hometown permanently, changing almost everything in your life.

As you transition, family and friends may also move away, bringing additional adjustments. These changes will require you to be open to developing new friendships and new interests.

Changes in the economy, past – present – future, also require lifestyle adjustments. Some of you who have already retired may need to go back to work. Others who have been laid off are now job hunting. These changes represent a few areas of your life that are impacted daily by uncertainty.

Getting Ready For This Transition

This is what you can expect to occur. The shift will be subtle but recognizable. You will begin to feel a restlessness that is laced with fear and uncertainty but also with excitement. You will find yourself thinking increasingly of the important life changes that will be a necessary part of your not-so-distant future. Rest assured that these are normal reactions to any transition. However, they may feel more exaggerated when you transition from traditional work to retirement.

Whether we are watching a movie or reading a book, we all recognize the familiar format. All stories start with a beginning, progress through to a middle stage, and finish with an ending. This all feels so reasonable and natural that it would be easy to try to apply this format to retirement. Retirement, however, is probably the exception that proves the rule.

Retirement almost always comes after a very long period of work. Thirty, forty, even fifty plus years is a very long time to be doing something every day which you then suddenly stop. No other transition in our life has worked this way. We were only in high school for four years before we transitioned to college or other training. We were only in college for four to six years before we moved into the workforce. Other transitions, like getting married and starting a family, occurred over relatively short periods of time. These other transitions also occurred when we were younger and much more flexible.

What also made these earlier transitions easier was that there was a script that everyone seemed to be following. When we were in high school, we all had older siblings or friends who were already in college or learning a trade. When we were in college, we were familiar with people several years older than us who were already in the workforce. At virtually every stage of our development, we had a multitude of examples of what our life would probably look like several years later. Everybody always had a pretty good idea about what they were supposed to be doing!

Retirement is clearly a different animal. The scripts that most of us are familiar with often seem old and out of place. Furthermore, there are no parents, teachers, advisors, instructors, supervisors, spouses, or even children who are telling us what our next move should be. There is no blueprint for how to build this next phase of our life! After a lifetime of hard work we finally arrive at a place where no one can tell us what to do. We are free to do anything that we want to do. But exactly what is that?

Ideally, an individual should start planning for retirement three to five years before their actual retirement date. The reason for this is so that we can put the ending first. As illogical as it sounds, retirement is that time in your life when the normal order of things is reversed. First comes the Ending, then the Neutral Zone, and finally the New Beginning.

In his two books entitled <u>Transitions</u> and <u>The Way of Transition</u>, William Bridges says that every life transition actually begins as an ending. He describes this process in three separate stages:

1. The Ending, letting go of what used to be.

2. The Neutral Zone, filled with uncertainty and self-exploration.

3. The New Beginning, finding clarity for what comes next.

As you face the realization that life as you have known it for many decades will change, you are faced with what you will do about it. You know you are longing for something different in the next part of your life. You also fantasize that this could be the beginning of a life shift that is truly unique and that this next phase of your life could be better than all of the rest.

The Ending Of What Used To Be

If you are reading this, you have already progressed through most of the well-defined stages of life: growing up in your family, finishing twelve years of compulsory education, going off to college or training, starting your career, getting married, creating a family, and climbing up the corporate ladder or starting your own business. Every transition you have gone through has required you to leave one stage of your life to begin the next stage. Throughout this lifelong journey, you made countless choices, explored and took advantage of many resources, and experienced many examples of what each life stage looks like to those who have gone before you.

Like every other transition, leaving your career where you have a clearly defined role to being retired or semi-retired requires that you end your work life as you have always known it. When you become intellectually and emotionally aware of this necessary shift from work, you will experience thoughts, feelings, and behaviors resulting from your decision to retire. It is common to experience the stages of grieving during this stage of the transition. These feelings signal that you are moving into the middle stage of this transition.

The Middle Stage: Disorientation To Reorientation

The middle stage of this transitional process is usually a time of exploration and can be filled with much uncertainty. When you retire or semi-retire, you may become less motivated to plan because the future is so unclear to you. What will you do in this stage of life? What will your day look like? How will you define yourself without work? How will you stay connected to and engaged with the friends you have enjoyed for a lifetime?

To compound the uncertainty, there are few positive role models to light the way. Unlike previous stages, this stage of life holds few "shoulds" or "have tos." It contains incomplete road maps and only vague blue prints. There is no one telling you what they expect of you or what you need to be planning for. As a result, it is normal to experience a variety of conflicting feelings about this change. Fear, confusion, uncertainty, anxiety, irritability, along with excitement and eagerness are emotions and feelings that are normal in this transition.

During this middle stage, the goal is to develop ways of dealing with these future changes in a productive and creative way. I have heard this stage referred to as the "fertile void." You'll find yourself considering new activities, careers, and doing research on your ideas and interests. If you haven't asked for assistance before you begin this retirement transition, this will be a good time to reach out for support from someone who can help guide you through this complicated yet exciting process. With professional support and encouragement in creating a foundation for this life transition, the ending may feel more complete and there may be a brighter light shining the way to a new beginning. It is important to take good care of yourself during this stage. *The middle stage is a great place to visit, but you wouldn't want to live there.*

The New Beginning

Once you have been able to progress through the middle stage of the transitional process, you will begin to create the time and space for something new. Bridges says there are two indications you are moving in the right direction.

1. The first is the reaction of those around you who see that the process has changed you and you are not simply repeating old predictable behaviors.

2. The second is being honest with yourself in having moved through the first two stages, which include an ending of your work career and the middle stage of exploring alternatives. You are then open to the realization that you are now ready for something new.

Here are some ways Bridges suggests that you can move into your new beginning:

1. Stop getting ready, which can become a loop of endless preparation, and *just do it,* whatever "it" turns out to be for you. In other words, don't be afraid to take a chance. If you have moved through the first and second stages, you have already reduced the risk factor.

2. Begin to identify with the final results of your new beginning. What will it feel like after you have actually done it? Will you be starting a new business, volunteering for a cause that you feel passionate about, or moving to a new town that fits your lifestyle better?

3. Create a plan that allows you to move step by step without being diverted from your path. Stay focused, gather information, and get support.

4. Enjoy the process without becoming obsessed by the goal.

Life transitions and especially moving into retirement can be a wonderful opportunity to grow from the inside out. Knowing yourself and being patient through this uncharted territory are necessary for a new beginning that reflects who you truly are. Stay focused on the fact that you are worth it! Take your time, get support, and make this transition the most successful one of your life.

Embracing Life in The Face Of Age

AARP The Magazine featured an article entitled "Aging's Not Optional." The article was about a group of AARP editors who attended a Bruce Springsteen concert at Giants Stadium. A woman, who was also attending, saw that they were wearing AARP T-shirts and asked, "Why would you wear an AARP T-shirt to a Springsteen concert?" A member of the group explained that they were editors of the largest circulation magazine for people over fifty and that Bruce Springsteen was himself sixty years old. The woman replied with a smile, "But why would you want people to know that you're really old?" This woman herself was in her sixties.

I chuckled as I read on because the author of the article, AARP editor Nancy Graham, said that she wanted to yell out, "I am as old as hell and I'm not going to take this anymore!" I loved it! The wisdom and experience that we have gathered has a great deal of value, and these gifts can only be received through years of living life. So why should we feel negative and self-conscious about our age?

This attitude has been referred to as "chronologically impaired" and, whether held by others or ourselves, can have a devastating impact on our outlook as we age. How about changing this mindset to feeling "chronologically gifted"?

Changing Our Mindset

Our personal view of aging, in turn, has a dramatic effect on our view of retirement. This is because the two of them are often thought to be cause and effect. When we are older, we retire, end of story. But what if we could un-think the two? How could we then change our attitude about both aging and retirement?

First, let's look at retirement alone. I believe the concept of retirement can be uncomfortable because it reminds each of us that we're no longer thirty-five years old. The pursuit of staying young is one of the main reasons that many people proudly proclaim that they'll never retire.

Many feel retirement is only for the older set, but back in the 80s and 90s, many dot-comers retired in their forties! Some retired to a traditional retirement and some to a whole new career adventure. So why is age a factor in retirement? It doesn't need to be. Anyone can retire at any age if they've planned exceptionally well. If we consider retirement as simply a point in our lives where we make a significant change from our current daily work life, it can take on a whole new and more positive meaning.

Now, let's look at aging itself. How we approach aging and how we take care of ourselves over time makes the difference in how well we can pursue *any* of our goals in later life, including retirement. Keeping active mentally, physically, and socially is key. That old adage "you are only as old as you feel" is more than a catchy phrase.

Unfortunately, chronological prejudice can creep into our lives, leaving us feeling negative. American culture, especially for those of us who came of age in the 60s and 70s, contains an onslaught of negativity toward aging. Just consider the continual focus of magazines and various articles over the past few decades on American's obsession with the youth culture. You know the ones that say something like "50 is the new 40"or "70 is the new 60."The point of all these articles is "Don't change!" We must stay young, healthy, and live forever, obviously achieving the impossible. Luckily, more recent times have brought a more realistic and acceptable societal attitude toward aging. The more we can focus on the positive, instead of this prejudice towards aging, the more positive our own attitude will be.

I'm not saying that aging doesn't give me pause. I definitely see changes going on in my world physically, emotionally, and socially. My career has evolved, and friendships have changed. My face has well-earned wrinkles, and my body parts are losing the battle with gravity. Many of my friends, colleagues, and family also reflect on the physical and social changes that we are experiencing as we age. Some of these aches, pains, and changes caused by aging are certainly more than an annoyance. However, it's all part of the life process. Most of the time, I am successful at embracing these changes and wonder how I will feel about it the same time next year.

How Aging Causes Resistance To Retirement

Once you un-think aging and retirement and view them for their own individual potential, you also need to recognize when the two do affect each other. As you age, some of your resistance to retirement isn't always conscious. The aging process itself makes many of us less accepting of change. Many people, perhaps you included, are most comfortable when everything stays the same. You found your "groove" and tend to resist anything that may upset that routine, including retirement. You also hold tightly to what makes you feel successful, happy, or fulfilled. In many cases, it's the job you know and have done for a period of your life as well as the routines you established in your work and social life. It's also the friends you enjoyed, and the organizations you joined. These are all good things. Transitioning to retirement brings change to many aspects of your life, and therefore has the potential to upset or at least change your groove.

You may continue to work solely so you can hold on to who you used to be. However, instead of allowing these inevitable life changes to create further resistance to your already established disposition against change, try embracing this life transition! This stage presents wonderful opportunities for new, fulfilling experiences. Everyone should consider this thought: how old would you feel if you didn't know how old you were? Don't let a number hold you back.

My Challenge To You

There are ways in which you can shift your mindset toward a more positive outlook about aging and retirement. Some suggestions:

1. Take care of you

Having a healthy body in retirement helps us live longer. Start now and exercise on a daily basis. In the book <u>Younger Next Year: Live Strong, Fit, and Sexy—Until You're 80 and Beyond</u> by Chris Crowley and Henry Lodge, MD, the authors say exercise improves longevity, overall health, mood, attitude, and the quality of your life as you age.

2. Celebrate the positive

Make a list of all the things you like about yourself and celebrate them. Work on accepting those things you don't like but can't change and change those things you can. Remember retirement, as well as life, is all about adapting to change. Adaptability keeps you thinking and acting younger.

3. Make your Bucket List

Write your own Life List or Bucket List of goals you want to accomplish before you leave this world. Work your way through the list. Research indicates that those who are the happiest in life, especially in retirement, have specific goals in mind and act on them.

4. Stay connected

As you transition from work, make sure you create a social network of loyal and sincere friends and family who support you in your life goals. People age with more grace when they are socially connected and engaged in life on a daily basis.

5. Embrace wisdom

Seek out intellectual stimulation and learn new skills even if it's uncomfortable. Stay engaged in life with a variety of activities.

Enjoy and remember: *you're only as old as you feel*, and you won't feel old if you stay actively engaged in life for the rest of your life.

Your Body And Retirement

What kind of relationship do you have with your body? This is an important question to ask at any time of our life, but especially as we transition to retirement. Are you kind and respectful toward your body because it is the only one you have or do you disregard signs and symptoms that there is something wrong? The question we all need to ask ourselves is: have we taken good care of our bodies? It reminds me of that funny quote by Mickey Mantle, "If I knew I'd live this long, I would have taken better care of myself." Those who enter the retirement stage of life with good health practices have a more successful retirement than those who have not developed and maintained positive health practices.

The generation that retired before the 1940s to 1950s often retired because they were not physically able to continue to work. To make things even worse, many retired to a life of limited intellectual and physical activity. Many believed that, because of a limited life expectancy, they wanted to concentrate on relaxing and having fun. In those previous generations, there was no definition of what a well-balanced retirement looked like. No one was concerned with long-term emotional, intellectual, and physical self-care and there was little information about health practices. Staying physically fit for life has only been emphasized since the mid-1960s when most baby boomers were entering high school. Prior to that time, many assumed that you stopped working, grew old, became sick, and then died.

Our Body, Past, Present, And Future

In the mid-1960s, Jim Fixx brought running into the mainstream of the physical fitness movement. He made people aware of the importance of exercising. I was a part of the running movement. Our running group ran inside because it wasn't stylish to run at all. As time went on, it made better sense to run outside, even in inclement weather. The concept of running and walking was so novel that friends and neighbors often slowed down in their cars to offer me a ride. Many families during that era did not know (nor were they encouraged) to exercise, eat a healthy diet, and get frequent medical checkups. Being Italian, I enjoyed the cultural ritual of large meals with many food choices and sitting around the table after a meal to relax and talk. I still enjoy parts of that ritual. However, you cannot live that lifestyle for long without feeling the consequences. For me, running gave me a heightened awareness of the benefits of exercise, health care including nutrition, life in moderation, and good medical care.

In 1987, after running for over twenty years, I realized the frequency and duration of my running was causing physical problems that were interfering with the quality of my life. As a result, I transitioned to walking while adding weight-bearing exercises. This has been my routine since then, with biking and swimming added periodically. It is true that how we have treated our bodies in the past will determine, for the most part, how our bodies will treat us in the future. That pattern of behavior will follow us into our later years as we retire. The consequences of some genetic diseases can even be minimized as we care for our health and learn to live with these challenges.

Positive Health Practices In Retirement

It is not too late, at any stage in life, to begin to take better care of your body. We can choose to start today and prevent serious health problems that will follow us into retirement or we can choose not to take action. It is totally up to us. It is important to acknowledge that our bodies do change with age. However, we can slow that process down with positive health care and healthy nutrition. Those practices include and are not limited to:

- Getting enough rest
- Eating well-balanced and nutritious meals
- Exercising after receiving your doctor's okay
- Not smoking or using drugs
- Moderate use of alcohol
- Balancing work and leisure

- Resolving life situations that are causing emotional and physical stress
- Managing stress in a healthy way: meditation, good friendship support, exercise, laughter
- Getting yearly medical checkups
- Managing a chronic illness with regular medical monitoring, acceptance, and a positive attitude

Wellness In Retirement

Wellness is more than maintaining good physical health. Wellness, from my perspective, includes not only your physical well-being but your emotional, social, and spiritual well-being. This is a holistic approach to living well regardless of the stage of life we are in. As each one of us transitions towards retirement, we will experience aches and pains after many years of the good life and, in some cases, the not-so-good life. Unfortunately, others may be experiencing more difficult challenges such as diabetes, cancer, high blood pressure, multiple sclerosis, etc. However, no matter what the circumstances, there are ways that you can manage these situations in order to minimize the impact these illnesses have on the quality of your life.

Living With Chronic Illness

What if you are living with a chronic illness or are diagnosed with one in your later years? Do you have enough emotional and physical reserves to adjust to the challenges of an illness? Many of the answers to these questions lie in your individual attitudes, lifestyle choices, support systems, and self-care rituals. We all have many internal and external resources if we only know how to tap into them.

I am amazed at the number of people I know who live very productive lives while dealing with major illnesses or diseases. My family members, mentioned earlier, are some of those people. Many have lived with these hardships for years, in some cases since childhood. For example, diabetes requires multiple blood glucose checks per day, a diet limiting sugar and carbohydrates, and frequent medical checkups. Cancer requires treatments like chemotherapy, radiation, or surgery and constant monitoring through the remainder of one's life. Yet many people handle these challenges well and are able to navigate the complicated side effects of these diseases that develop as they age. Unfortunately, others are never quite able to accept their illness or are unable to integrate it into their self-care routine, leaving them with negative unresolved emotions about their illness.

Attitudes Towards Wellness

We can probably all agree that it isn't what happens to us, but how we react to life's events that will most affect their outcome. Years ago, I sustained a back injury while running in a race. The results of this annoying but not serious injury have stayed with me even though I have tried numerous treatments along with surgery. I have come to accept my back problem as a chronic condition I will have to live with until there is a more effective treatment or better surgery. I have minimized my discomfort from this chronic condition with aerobic exercise, strength training, physical therapy, yoga, acupuncture, and meditation.

How many times have you gone to bed feeling badly about something physical or emotional, with no end in sight? Yet by morning you had a better perspective on the situation. I can think of many times over the years where I may have been discouraged or confused about a situation. However, by talking to a friend or colleague, meditating, or just waiting a day or two, I have been able to arrive at clarity along with a more positive attitude about it.

Regardless of what you are facing, your attitude is a key factor in how successful you can cope with life challenges. I was so impressed by the positive attitude of the woman who lost both of her legs in the senseless Boston Marathon bombing in spring of 2013. She wasn't feeling sorry for herself, but expressed her desire to move forward with physical therapy and get her prostheses so she could get on with her life. This tragedy was not going to define the rest of her life.

Finding Your Wellness Practices

Since there are bound to be unpleasant events in your life, especially as you age, what are some ways that you can be better prepared to face them? I sincerely hope you will work through the Dig Deeper questions and make changes in your life where necessary.

Dig Deeper

Do you see yourself as "chronologically gifted," not "chronologically impaired"?

Do you have the support you need in your life from your family and friends?

Are you free from regrets about the past? What needs to happen to release them?

Can you laugh at yourself and not sweat the small stuff?

Have you resolved emotional conflicts and made amends where necessary?

Are you able to accept change? If not, what needs to happen to "change" that?

Do you see your glass as half full? If not, how can you make it fuller?

If you answered "no" to any of these questions, which one will you work on first?

What are three steps you can take this week toward answering "yes" to the question?

Retirement Resources

Books

The Creation Of Health: The Emotional, Psychological, And Spiritual Responses That Promote Health And Healing by Caroline Myss and C. Norman Shealy

The Way Of Transition: Embracing Life's Most Difficult Moments by William Bridges

Transitions: Making Sense Of Life's Changes by William Bridges

Younger Next Year: Live Strong, Fit, and Sexy—Until You're 80 and Beyond by Chris Crowley and Henry Lodge

Web Sites

AARP and health

http://www.aarp.org/health

Check your health

http://www.realage.com

Take charge of your healthcare

http://www.healthfinder.gov

Wellness resources

http://www.wellness.com

Chapter 5

Be On The Winning Team

"Even though it's at the end of the season and we are on the outside looking in, we are still playing together and it shows you there is no quit in this team."

Rashard Lewis

Is Your Marriage Or Relationship Ready For Retirement?

It is complicated and challenging enough to think about retirement for ourselves, but it is even more challenging for couples to plan for retirement. There are many complex retirement needs that are unique to living with a spouse or partner. To have a successful retirement, each spouse needs to be able to compromise and cooperate with understanding and empathy while still maintaining their own autonomy in a relationship.

My Success Is Not Your Success

The way we navigate this next stage of our lives will be a very personal process because it requires introspection, thoughtful planning, communication, and cooperation if you are a part of a couple. What defines success in retirement for you may not be the same for your spouse or partner. How will you handle the challenges of this reality as you look forward to slowing down and taking time to explore what will bring you purpose, meaning, and satisfaction? Some spouses might be looking for variety, intellectual stimulation, and travel while the other spouse might be more interested in physical activities, hobbies, and more social stimulation. What process will help you find a common thread to weave together the different interests that you might have into a tapestry that reflects who both of you are together and separately?

Where To Live

Couples sometimes differ regarding where to live permanently or where to buy a second home, and these differences may create conflict. As the time nears to make a decision, an impasse may develop without warning. I know of several couples who have struggled with this decision, and my husband and I are one of them.

Tom and I have always been good communicators about many issues and challenges that have come up over the years but when the time came to buy a second home, I found out something I had not known about him. During some of his college undergraduate years, he had enjoyed living in the city environment of Baltimore, Maryland. Fresh out of college as a young engineer, he had hopes of continuing to live in the city, enjoying that lifestyle. However, because he and his first wife decided to start a family, they thought it would be best to move from a city apartment to the suburbs.

When we began to think about what we wanted in our retirement, I realized he still romanticized about the city environment with the fast-paced, interesting attractions and the 24/7 excitement a city offers. I, on the other hand, wanted to be by the beach or by some body of water because that is what I find relaxing. However, we did agree on one thing and that was we both wanted a warm climate! As we talked more about what each of us wanted and began to explore the options, it became clearer what would really work best for us, and we began to look for it.

Making A Decision

Initially, we had no idea how our choice would turn out but we continued to talk, respecting what the other needed. We made a number of trips to Florida before we found a condo in downtown Tampa that overlooks Tampa Bay. We have a dramatic view of the city skyline and the waters of Tampa Bay.

Fortunately, the entire process was a positive experience and we had a happy ending. I am now also enjoying the benefits of being in a city along with the water views that I truly enjoy. The beach which was my first choice is only twenty-five minutes away, and we go there often. Tom, on the other hand, loves to watch all of the activity in the harbor and ride around the city on his motorcycle, sometimes with me in tow.

Some spouses may want to be closer to friends and family, while others may want to try a new environment. Some spouses may want to travel while others like to be at home where things are familiar. Many couples will have differences about whether to move to the beach, the mountains, a lake, the river, or the desert. The main goal is to go to a place where both of you can feel comfortable and fulfilled. The challenge is to find a compromise so that both of your needs can be met as best as possible. This only happens when you keep the communication open and keep a shared vision in sight.

Over the years I have had many opportunities to help couples talk with each other in healthier ways, hear what each other wants, and share understanding and empathy for each other's needs. These are important skills in the discussions you will have during this phase of life if you are married.   The keys to a successful marriage and a successful retirement for couples are love, intimacy, communication, mutuality, commitment, trust, and respect. Your relationship needs to be nurtured throughout your whole life, especially in retirement when you will be spending more time together.

Caring For Your Relationship Into Retirement

Recently, I overheard a man say he wasn't going to buy his wife anything for Valentine's Day because he shows her he loves and appreciates her every day. I hope what he said was true but his comment made me think about the importance of love and romance throughout marriage, and especially as a couple prepares for retirement.

Attraction

Men and women are attracted to each other for many reasons. Some of the factors are physical attraction, chemistry, intelligence, the ability to laugh and have fun, kindness, and dependability. Similarities in our personalities, interests and values also attract you to your partner. But should you overlook that old adage that opposites attract? Good question. Introverts often attract extroverts, early birds attract night owls, a serious person might be attracted to a partner who is funny, and an intellectual may be attracted to someone who is emotionally expressive.

What happens is that during the course of the relationship, a healthy couple deepens their love, commitment, understanding, trust, and respect because of and in spite of these differences. That is because a healthy couple can stretch into behavior changes at their own pace. Their differences do not disappear but a couple can grow closer together with healthy communication as a result of those differences. Here's how it works. Some who have a characteristic within themselves that is not developed try to find that part in their partner. This helps to create the attraction but it can also create conflict. For example, one partner might have a strong emotional reaction to certain situations while the other is great at thinking the problem through without emotion.

If two people stay polarized with their emotional versus intellectual approach, chronic conflict arises. However, if the feeling spouse increases their ability to express thoughts and ideas while the thinking spouse works on developing the capacity to feel and be sensitive to the other's feelings, their relationship will feel safer and they become a better team in managing conflict and solving problems. Couples unwilling or unable to change often experience resentments and their individual needs remain unfulfilled. Growth comes when each person can develop in themselves what they admire most in the other. What attracted you to your spouse? How can you sustain and deepen that attraction into your golden years?

What Helps A Marriage Last?

I attended a lecture by Charles and Elizabeth Schmitz, the Marriage Doctors, who talked about their book <u>Golden Anniversaries: The Seven Secrets of Successful Marriage</u>. This book is based on twenty-five years of research where they interviewed couples all over the world who had been married for at least thirty years. They asked each couple what had sustained their long-term marriage. The summary of the couples' responses are as follows:

- Take time to reconnect with each other after retirement and get to know one another again.
- Be careful not to fall into the habit of sitting and watching television or doing other passive activities. Plan what you want to do with this time and be creative and active.
- Balance time together while also respecting private time to be alone. Reflect and pursue individual interests.
- Build a social network of friends and stay active and connected to family.
- Be willing to be spontaneous along with having activities planned during your day and week.
- Support and encourage positive health practices in your marriage and care for each other when ill.
- Share a mutual respect and support for the financial integrity of your marriage.

How You Can Nurture Your Marriage Into Retirement

So what creates the conditions for both a long-term and healthy marriage? Regardless of the length of a marriage, the significant word in the previous sentence is "healthy." After all, some marriages last a long time but they are not very healthy. Integrating my own personal perspective, professional training, and experience as a couples' therapist along with the research mentioned above, I surveyed some couples I know who have had healthy, long-term marriages. The following additional qualities emerged as sustaining a marriage into retirement:

- Honesty, respect, and trust
- Having a sense of humor and having fun together
- Having a willingness to work on your marriage in the face of challenges
- Listening with curiosity to your spouse's point of view without judgment because there is always more to learn if you ask the right questions
- Appreciating your partner at least once a day for something they have done or for a quality you admire in them
- Liking each other as friends as well as being lovers and saying "I love you"
- Remembering that love is a verb, so share affection and other caring behaviors
- Sharing common interests, values, desires, and a mutual vision for the future

- Going on weekly dates with each spouse taking turns choosing the place or activity to keep it interesting and surprising
- Communicating clearly and honestly when discussing something you may disagree on then making sure you reflect back what you heard before responding to confirm you understand your partner
- Doing an annual evaluation of your marriage vision and deciding if you want to make some changes moving forward

As a result of the Marriage Doctors' research and my couples' responses to the question about a long-lasting and healthy marriage, I would like to invite you to integrate some of these practices into your marriage. It is never too late to breathe healthy energy, excitement, love, and romance into your marriage or relationship. Experience the changes in your marriage and enjoy the benefits of these suggestions now and into your retirement years.

How To Avoid Becoming A Divorce Statistic

We all know couples who have been married for many years and who have decided to divorce. After a lifetime of communicating about day-to-day events, parenting, and career aspirations, somehow their communication and their connection broke down. A Cornell study revealed that married couples struggle with being retired for the first two years. Many are not prepared for the relational changes that occur.

More recently, The National Center for Family and Marriage Research at Bowling Green State University found that at least one in four marriages of those fifty and older are ending in divorce. They even have a name for this trend; it's called "Gray Divorce." How can we avoid becoming a part of this statistic?

I want to share some thoughts about the influences retirement has on marriage and how to cope with the significant changes this transition brings.

Responding To Relationship Challenges

As a psychotherapist and coach, I have worked predominantly with boomers in my career. You might say we've grown up together. In the early years, I noticed women were the ones responsible for initiating therapy, either for themselves, for their children, or for their marriages. This made sense because they were usually the ones attending to and nurturing the emotional environment of the family. Many of these women's concerns focused on the well-being of the family and trying to balance the pressures of family life and careers. As a couple focuses on day-to-day needs, these stresses can result in couples not having or taking the time to talk to each other and nurture their marriages. This disconnect can ultimately lead to parallel relationships where the connection is fractured or lost.

Interestingly, over the last decade, I have noticed men have been more willing to ask for support as they move into their fifties and sixties. They seem to have developed more emotional awareness about the needs of their families as well as their relationships and are looking at the next stage of their lives with questions, concerns, and an awareness that the family is changing. They see their children getting older and going off to college or careers. Both spouses also observe their parents aging, often being called on to support their needs. By their early to mid-fifties, these changing dynamics frequently find boomers sandwiched between their children who have not yet left home and their aging parents, who increasingly need help.

Many have reached their career goals and seem satisfied with where they are. Now they are looking at their marriage and wondering what it is going to look like as they grow older together. This can challenge any relationship but especially if they haven't maintained their connection.

Strengthening Your Team Effort

In the first part of marriage, spouses' roles are more clearly defined than they are as couples approach retirement. As couples are freed from their child-rearing and career building stages, they begin to think about how their roles will change going forward. The first thing couples need to realize is that retirement has a way of rearranging a couple's relationship. Women, who have often sacrificed their needs for the good of their family, want additional time and opportunities to explore new interests. When women re-career, they are also more financially secure, independent, and confident in their abilities to support themselves. Men, on the other hand, are expecting more time with their wives because they are not working long hours away from home.

This is the time for couples to come together to plan for this next stage of their lives. Decisions regarding how to handle money, domestic responsibilities, maintaining autonomy, whether to move or stay in place, and how to maintain separate as well as common friendships and interests are only a few of the discussions necessary for a successful transition to retirement.

Fine Tuning Your Relationship

Brown University professor Rose McDermott's interpretation of relationships tracked in the Framingham (Massachusetts) Heart Study captured international attention. According to researchers, divorce in one's immediate circle of friends can increase the chances you, too, will divorce by up to 75%. Statistics are lower but still significant for co-worker and geographically distant siblings who divorce.

So you won't become a statistic, here are some suggestions to begin now to nurture your relationship as you prepare for this next life stage:

- Begin planning for this transition at least three to five years before you actually retire.
- Set aside at least one hour a week to begin discussing what decisions you will be making around the various life arenas: career, finances, family, personal growth, leisure, self-care.

- Communicate not only by talking but also by listening with an open mind and an open heart.
- Each partner should write down what was discussed and keep an ongoing journal of decisions they've made, additional topics to be discussed, and some of the feelings they have about these decisions.
- Be willing to stretch into new roles or shared roles to keep your relationship strong and your skill set versatile.
- Make sure that you get help if the foundation of your marriage has been impacted by a parallel relationship. A parallel relationship is when two people who live together aren't emotionally connected to one another, have lost the ability to be in touch, yet still love each other. My experience has been that if people wait too long to get that support, it is harder for them to reconnect.

Life is too short and your relationship history is too long to give up easily. Some marriages should have ended long ago and can't be worked out but most have strong potential to succeed. Make sure you give your relationship a good chance towards success.

Love The One You're With And The Dreams They Aspire To

Let's talk about the importance of having the loving support from your significant other as you explore your dreams and turn them into goals. As you begin planning the transition to retirement, numerous conversations will be necessary to create a successful, fulfilling, and happy lifestyle. Sharing your hopes, dreams, and aspirations for this new life stage with your partner is an extremely important aspect of achieving success. Where you will live, what you will spend money on, what kind of activities you will do separately and together, and how you take care of your health are all important topics of the conversation. Within each of these areas there are undoubtedly hopes and dreams you may not have shared with each other.

To illustrate this point, I would like to share this quote by Gail Devers: "Keep your dreams alive. Understand to achieve anything requires faith and belief in yourself, vision, hard work, determination, and dedication. Remember all things are possible for those who believe."

Discussing your dreams is harder than you think! Before having a conversation with your partner, you need to be organized and extremely honest with yourself.

- What do you really want in your life?
- What values will guide your decisions?
- Do you have the skills as a couple to navigate the tough conversations where you may have disagreements about your future life dreams and goals?
- How will you handle ideas and feelings from your partner that are different from your own?

The challenge for each of us as we face conflicting values and ideas is to arrive at an acceptable compromise. Whether your partner wants to do an archaeological dig in Egypt or start his or her own business, providing support in a nonjudgmental way is important to finding a practical compromise. I would like to offer some specific tips that may help you on this journey of discovery so you can cooperate in a caring and loving way and avoid the possibility that you may stifle your partner's dreams.

1. Practice the art of communication. It is vital to a healthy relationship and the dreams you and your partner aspire to. If left unspoken, these dreams will never happen. Taking the time to talk about your hopes and dreams sets the tone for the importance of these conversations. Talk clearly about your desires and ask for support as you explore what you have always dreamed of doing but were afraid to try. Ask your partner to let you know what they're hearing you say. As you have these conversations, quietly listening is just as important as talking as your partner shares their thoughts and feelings. Ask questions. How long has that dream been there waiting to be revealed? How important is this dream and how will it change your life? When you are listening attentively without judgment, it is safer for your partner to share more openly. Be respectful of your partner's thoughts and feelings and expect the same in return. You will be surprised at what you learn about the person you love. You will certainly be motivated to find a way to support your loved one's dreams. *You will be sharing the language of love.*

2. Make a commitment to your dreams. Doing what you've always dreamed of doing will only happen if you have the courage to commit to taking the steps necessary to make it happen. Ask for your partner's understanding, cooperation and support for your dreams. It is important to have a supportive partner, along with trusted friends, to hold you accountable for your actions. Imagine how much you could learn from each other as you have conversations that are open and honest. What are the steps necessary to realize your dream? In addition to the support of your partner, will you need to save money over time, research possibilities, look for a support group, or find a mentor? Explore how your different aspirations can be merged or compromised in a cooperative way. As you work towards your dream, *commitment will be experienced as loving support, and then you can celebrate together!*

3. Gather information as you explore your dreams, and ask your partner to listen to you as you explore ideas out loud. Find out what others have done to realize similar goals. Search the Web. Sometimes a good friend or partner is better at research than you are. They can support you by helping you gather information. Even if the dream is beyond reach for whatever reason, having an intimate partner discover alternative ways of realizing this dream has great value. *By exploring together, you will deepen your loving connection.*

4. Be adventuresome as you explore your dreams. Taking risks requires that you get out of your comfort zone. Stretch. Learn new skills. Brainstorm possibilities and go for it if both of you are in agreement that this dream is feasible. If not, modify the dream, but don't give up on it. On the Civic Ventures Website, I read recently about a doctor who had retired to leisure—playing golf. Unsatisfied with this lifestyle he thought he wanted, he now sets up non-profit clinics in various areas of the United States to help those in need of medical services. How adventuresome and generous is that? *Supporting adventure in your relationship is an act of love and generates positive energy, especially when you're doing it together.*

5. *Write it down to make it a viable dream.* My husband often tells me it is not a plan until you put it on paper. Without a written plan, goals are just words frozen forever in a dream state without the possibility of becoming a reality. What a loss of a great idea that could possibly change the world. Don't let that happen! Writing down your thoughts, ideas, and dreams to share with others has the benefit of crystallizing what is important to all involved. It is mutually beneficial.

By using these simple steps, you will have the opportunity to turn your dreams into achievable goals and help each other stretch, grow, and find purpose in life one dream at a time. What better way is there to build intimacy and fun into your relationship all year long?

Dig Deeper

What qualities do you value and need in your partner and other significant relationships?

What values will guide your decisions whether you are married or single?

Do you have the skills as a couple to navigate the tough conversations where you may have disagreements about your life dreams and goals?

How will you handle ideas and feelings from your partner that are different from your own?

How willing are you to negotiate differences and compromise as you converse with your partner?

What topics do you need to discuss to make important decisions?

What family relationships will be impacted by your retirement decisions?

Retirement Resources

Books

<u>Golden Anniversaries: The Seven Secrets Of Successful Marriage</u> by Charles and

Elizabeth Schmitz

<u>The Couples Retirement Puzzle: 10 Must-Have Conversations For Transitioning To The Second Half Of Life</u> by Roberta Taylor and Dorian Mintzer

Studies

Cornell Study on Couples

"The Gray Divorce Revolution" by Susan Brown and I-Fen Lin of Bowling Green State University, National Center for Family and Marriage Research

Chapter 6

Take Small Bites

"When eating an elephant take one bite at a time."

Creighton Abrams

Creating A Value-Based Retirement

We often hear people talk about values and what they feel is important to them. Values are consistent ideals that are personally important to each of us and give our life true meaning. We all have them, and many of us share common values that affect how we live our lives. As we transition into our retirement, it is not unusual to begin to explore questions like "What is really important to me?" "What are my values?" "How can I become more conscious of living my life, making sure my behaviors are in alignment with my values?" By acting consciously, one act at a time, you can be sure that living by your values in later years will reflect your life's true meaning and purpose.

What Are Your Core Values?

While doing my coach training at Coach University, one of the courses required us to do a Values Inventory Exercise. As I reflected back on this experience, I remember being impressed with the fact that this concept was explored, inventoried, and then discussed among our training group. For the first time, I looked carefully at this list and quickly identified those I was currently living by. This exercise is something that many of us do unconsciously, but this process brought it to a whole different level for me. For illustrative purposes, here are some of the values I strive to live by:

- Appreciating relationships with family and friends and experiencing a sense of community
- Having high standards in my personal and professional life
- Volunteering my time and contributing to my community through Rotary membership and other groups
- Supporting, teaching, and encouraging others
- Life-long learning of new skills, concepts, and activities
- Sustaining a healthy lifestyle by exercising, eating well, and getting enough rest

What values would you list? Are you currently living by those values or do you need to look more closely at this aspect of your life? Who in your life is modeling core values you might like to incorporate into your life?

Aligning Your Values With Your Lifestyle

As a therapist as well as a life and retirement coach, I explore these issues with my clients. I have used this exercise as a foundation for discussions about what is truly important to them. Are your life goals, planning behaviors, ideas, and projects in alignment with your core values? If not, you may experience difficulty generating the energy it takes to reach your goals, complete a project, or stay with an idea. You may be headed in a direction that will lead to a less satisfying transition if that hasn't happened already.

For example, if you value family and friends yet you plan to move far away from them, will you be truly happy in your retirement? Relocating is always a reasonable choice as long as you can make visits back to your roots and have friends and family visit you in your new home. This can work well until you establish new relationships in your new environment. I call this phasing into your new lifestyle.

Some say they value their health and will start to make changes when they are no longer working and have the time. If this truly is a value, isn't it time now to start making those lifestyle changes that will lead you to your goal of having a healthier body?

My Challenge To You

I encourage you to explore your core values and determine what is important to you. What will give your life meaning in your retirement, whether you are in that transition now or will be transitioning in the future? Take the Values Assessment at http://www.WhatsNext.com. Make a list of what is really important to you and then determine whether or not your current life reflects these values. Listen to your thoughts, feelings, and levels of motivation, and you will have the answer to whether or not your values are being honored by you and your lifestyle.

Life-Long Goals: Get What You Want When You Want It

I am always fascinated by people who make New Year's resolutions. It is as if there is only one time of year when you are supposed to make plans to change something in your life. It would benefit us all, as well as our families and communities, if we were setting goals and moving forward all year, every year.

Goals help us to stay engaged in life and connected with others. Discover what you feel drawn to and go with that flow to move forward throughout all of your life. Take small, continuous steps throughout your life instead of trying to achieve all of your life goals this year.

Although setting goals has served me well in my life, I am a little more relaxed about it than I used to be. My expectation is that goal setting will always be a part of who I am, and I want to help you explore the importance of setting realistic goals for yourself throughout all life stages.

The Profile Of A Boomer

I'm a boomer who turned sixty-five years old in 2011. Being post World War II babies, we have watched our parents—who grew up during the Great Depression— struggle and strive for a better life for themselves and their families. The things the "Greatest Generation" achieved are no less than phenomenal. As we observed, we learned it was our responsibility to work hard, continuing the progress our parents started. It could be said that this attitude became a part of our birthright. We worked hard and played hard and changed our environment whenever it was necessary.

As a result of our upbringing during these historic times, our generation tends to be high achieving and service oriented. As Leo Buscaglia said, "Each of our acts makes a statement as to our purpose. Most of us are willing to do whatever it takes to get the job done." A successful career has become a staple of our identity. For many of us, our legacy has been positive changes in civil rights and a desire for world peace. We have improved technology, raised profound awareness regarding multicultural and age-related diversity, feminism, sexuality, and the environment. For many boomers, turning fifty and sixty wasn't a downer but a positive milestone about what was next.

The Trap

Unfortunately, even though we have this extremely remarkable profile, our attitudes about retirement are still mainly rooted in the model our parents and grandparents retired with. After finding this model unsatisfactory, our generation is not willing to rest on the laurels of past accomplishments. Instead, you want to continue to change your world in positive ways.

So, why is it that some people, as they age, equate this life stage with just letting go and coasting on what they accomplished in the past? Don't fail to walk your talk.

This kind of thinking results in living more in the past, falling short of moving forward in a new way so you can continue your impressive legacy. I have seen this trend in a number of older people who have already retired. For some, it's hard to change a pattern when there isn't a new model to emulate. It is up to us, once again, to set the trend for this next phase of our lives so it will be much more fulfilling than we've seen in past generations. We will have many years to shakeup, change, and infuse energy into our generation's legacy, which will be left for future generations. What is the best way you can succeed in harnessing a new retirement model just as you have succeeded in transforming other life-changing movements?

A New Trend

Mark Twain wrote, "Twenty years from now, you will be more disappointed by the things that you didn't do than by the things that you did do. So throw off the bowlines. Sail away from the harbor. Catch the trade winds in your sails. Explore, dream, discover."

How will you explore, dream, and discover? What goals will you set for yourself in this stage of your life and in the future? What will give more meaning to your life and make you happier, more hopeful, and more satisfied?

A model I think works well for many of us is setting goals using the six areas of life we live in every day. They are:

- Work
- Self-care

- Finances
- Relationships
- Leisure
- Personal growth

Be SMART

You may be familiar with the SMART model for setting important goals, namely goals should be **S**pecific, **M**easurable, **A**chievable, **R**ealistic, and **T**ime-sensitive. Although this is a very effective model, C. A. Miller and M. B. Frisch, in their book entitled _Creating Your Best Life: The Ultimate Life List Guide_, added some extra components to this model to help people set goals for all life stages, especially in planning for retirement. Their book is filled with research and life examples supporting the reality that those who set goals throughout life are happier, healthier, and more successful than those who don't. Here are some additional characteristics for goal setting they identified. Goals should be:

- Challenging in order to make you stretch and grow
- Exciting and magnetic in order to draw you to what you feel passionate about
- Value-driven in order to reflect what's important to you
- Positive in order to create feelings of independence, connectedness, and competence
- Intrinsic and purposeful in order to motivate from within and give life meaning
- Written down in order to put it in black and white and keep it visible
- Reflect commitment and accountability in order to make a lasting difference to yourself and others

Goals help you stay engaged in life and keep you connected with others. Discover what you personally feel drawn to and go with that flow. Remember John Wooden's quote "Don't let what you cannot do interfere with what you can do."

Go ahead and set some SMART goals within each of the six areas of life. When you achieve one goal, set another to keep you moving in your chosen direction. In the process, you will be achieving my trademarked tagline, which is "making the best of your life for the rest of your life!"

Reconsidering Retirement Goals

In the fall of 2008, many of us were astonished by the unprecedented losses in the stock market, the uncertainty of the real estate market, and the extremely shaky economy. Are you thinking the solution to an economic downturn is to postpone your retirement for another five, ten, or even fifteen years? Wrong! The assumption that you need to totally postpone your plans because of the economy is based on a faulty premise that retirement is primarily "financially based," and if you had enough money, you could have a successful retirement. Conversely, the thinking goes that without all of the money you had originally planned for, there is no way you can retire. This belief is not only faulty but ignores the fact that more and more people want to continue working after they retire but not because of economic reasons. Boomers are setting a new precedent by making work, on their own terms, a part of their retirement portfolio.

Less Money Is Not The Problem, More Money Is Not The Solution

As mentioned in previous chapters, financial security is only one aspect of successful retirements. So much emphasis has been placed on money that, while many people retiring have adequate financial resources, they have no direction, no plan, no purpose, and no meaning to their lives. Each day looks just like the last. I have observed this, read about it, and heard people share their stories about this phenomenon for years.

Many adverse situations that begin as serious problems can actually create new opportunities in life. Why not turn a negative into a positive by using our present economic problems as an opportunity to reconsider what you had always planned for in your retirement years? Is moving to another location what is really best for you? Is stopping work completely your ultimate objective?

Maybe you could retire when you originally planned by thinking outside the box. When you created your original retirement plan, did you really know what you wanted? How many of us have made important decisions in the excitement of the moment, only to reflect back on them at a later time with regrets?

In Marc Freedman's book <u>Encore</u>, he describes people whose lives were destined for a traditional retirement to leisure. Through unexpected life circumstances—a downturn in the economy or setbacks they experienced in their work environment or personal life—everything changed. These individuals used the gift of adversity and the extra time to create opportunities that made a significant difference in their world. They experienced a more successful retirement than they had ever envisioned. It took stopping, re-evaluating, and changing direction to make this happen. After they re-examined their changed circumstances, they became determined not to use the next thirty years of their lives playing golf and getting lost in a leisurely life without purpose.

If you haven't carefully considered the non-economic aspects of this important life transition, then maybe a financial crisis is an opportune time to stop and reconsider your future. This effort could lead to an improvement of your original plan as it morphs into a whole new vision. The old adage from the 1960s mentioned earlier is as alive and well today as it was then: "failing to plan is planning to fail."

Many are working in retirement but doing it in a different way and doing something they truly love and enjoy. These people—although retired—have a lot to give and aren't simply looking for a paycheck. A number of companies are reaching out to retirees who have skills they now need and asking them to return to work, but this time with a more flexible schedule. How ideal!

What have you always wanted to do but didn't have the time or money to do? Is there a cause out there that could bring you some income but not tie you down and rob you of hard-earned free time? What was a dream you had when you were younger that you would like to pursue in retirement? These are the kinds of questions that could lead you down the path of self-discovery. Go ahead, lift your sails and let your dreams move you towards your life's purpose.

Dig Deeper

What values do you hold dear to you that guide your decision-making process?

Are you creating a values-based retirement plan for yourself with the values you have identified?

Does your retirement plan include all these areas?

- Work

- Self-care

- Finances

- Relationships

- Leisure

- Personal growth

What goals have you set for yourself in each of the areas above?

What cause out there could bring you some income but not tie you down and rob you of hard-earned free time?

What dream did you have when you were younger that you would like to pursue in retirement?

Retirement Resources

Books

Creating Your Best Life: The Ultimate Life List Guide by Caroline Miller and Michael Frisch

Encore: Finding Work That Matters In The Second Half Of Life by Marc Freedman

"Keeping A Foot In Both Worlds" by Sarah Halzack, the Washington Post, Capital Business, September 3-9, 2012

The Big Shift: Navigating The New Stage Beyond Midlife by Marc Freedman

Web Sites

Values assessment

http://www.whatsnext.com

Chapter 7

Have An Attitude Of Gratitude

"Develop an attitude of gratitude, and give thanks for everything that happens to you, knowing that every step forward is a step toward achieving something bigger and better than your current situation."

Brian Tracy

What Is Your Attitude Toward Retirement?

I have already admitted I was one of those boomers who was not terribly optimistic and positive about retirement. It was not initially clear to me why I felt that way, but I knew I did not want the retirement lifestyles I observed many others having, including my family and friends.

Experiencing some of those lifestyles from a distance made me want to hold on to my work. Part of that had to do with enjoying the work I had been doing for so many years. The other part had to do with the alternative of not having my life filled with purpose, social connections, and intellectual stimulation beyond my practice. I saw many of my older retired friends and family members losing some of these very important aspects of their lives. When I began looking at the statistics, I found that in an Internet poll of 130,000 people, 80% perceived aging as a downer. Of those 130,000 people, only 10,000 were over sixty years old. This poll piqued my interest, and I wondered why the concept of retirement as it relates to aging was negative for so many younger people. Where does this attitude come from, and are these statistics reflected in the feelings of people who have actually retired?

How Attitudes Are Formed—Role Models

Many attitudes are created by the role models we were exposed to when we were much younger. Our parents are usually our most influential role models as are other relatives and friends. We noticed how they talked about retirement, which revealed their feelings, attitudes, and prejudices about it. We then observed their actions as they actually made this transition. Some were satisfied with a retirement to leisure, while others became complacent and then depressed. How many stories have you heard about some people dying six months to a year after they retired? We have also heard how our older, retired friends and colleagues feel about this transition. Some, I noticed, retired with excitement about the prospect of a life filled with purpose and leisure. Others seemed to busy their lives with activities that just filled time. No wonder some people are not as fulfilled as they used to be and feel that there is something missing.

Social Influence

Without being fully aware of it, we are continuously bombarded by society's attitudes about retirement and aging. Many companies have policies that require us to retire at a certain age. People forced to retire early might feel they are no longer useful to society, and many will try to seek other employment. They are often unprepared when they encounter age discrimination. They are also fearful they might not be able to compete with a more youthful group willing to accept lower pay. This attitude, which can also reflect an employer's attitude, often minimizes the value of mentorship and wisdom residing within older workers who still have much more to give. Some retirees will find a way around this by effectively advocating for themselves. They realize they have experience and intellectual property most younger employees do not possess. Some have requested and received adjusted work schedules, while others enjoy volunteering, mentoring, or teaching to satisfy this need.

Media

The media also plays a crucial role in our attitudes as we see and hear ads for how to look younger and be healthier. They tantalize us with products that are supposed to erase all of our wrinkles so we can hold on to that youthful look. We earned those wrinkles and they reflect the wisdom and life experience we gathered along life's way. If you decide on any procedures, make sure you leave a few wrinkles. It's OK. There is nothing wrong with keeping up with the times, making the most of what you have, and taking good care of yourself. However, using extreme ways to hold on to the way we used to look or trying to recreate life the way it used to be may reflect something else going on.

Personality

Another important aspect affecting our attitudes towards retirement is the personality and disposition we bring to this transition. Is our glass half empty or half full? Do we look for alternatives when things don't go our way, or do we succumb to paralysis or victimization? Do we look for lessons in some of the trials, tribulations, and losses in life or do we feel defeated and accept a situation that could be very fertile ground for depression? Do we truly believe if we change our attitude, we can change our life? Are we self-reflective as we think and feel our way through a life event, or do we go through it without self-awareness and miss the larger picture? As we ponder retirement, we may not realize that all of these variables are actually influencing our current attitudes. How we approached other life stages will often affect how we feel about retirement.

As a retirement lifestyle coach, I am always interested in other people's lives to gain more insight about this transition. Several years ago, I was researching the lives of famous people when I read about George Eastman, founder of the Eastman Kodak Company. I was stunned and saddened to learn about the circumstances of Mr. Eastman's untimely death. Although he founded a world-class company, somehow he lost his positive attitude towards retirement. Two months after he retired in his mid-70s, he committed suicide and left a note that said, "My work is done, why wait?" What other wonderful inventions, businesses, and philanthropic contributions could he have made in his life? Unfortunately, we will never know.

An Attitude of Growth And Renewal

I want you to consider one more important thought so you can look at your retirement with a more positive attitude. This stage of life is free of the requirements of achieving academic degrees, moving up the corporate ladder, or raising a family. It leaves us with the gifts of time, freedom, wisdom, and insight. This is our opportunity to discover who we are underneath all of our roles, titles, and work responsibilities. Retirement is a journey, not a destination. Self-discovery should be an ongoing process for as long as we live.

Money And Retirement Satisfaction

Retirement is no different than other life stages when it comes to money. Over and over again, studies have shown that people with a lot of money are no happier and have just as many problems as those with less money. People who believe that the presence of money is the determining factor in their life satisfaction are often disappointed. Many of you know people who don't have a lot of money but are still satisfied and happy with their lives. Those people have usually found the satisfaction of having life purpose and meaning rather than materialistic satisfaction. Fortunately, purpose does have value in our lives.

The Gift Of Gratitude

You have probably heard about writing a gratitude list and adding to it daily. During rough times, I remember actively focusing on the positive aspects of my life and our marriage with gratitude. We were healthy, had wonderful families, a good support system, and we saw the potential for a great future. Throughout the bad times we shared our fears, disappointments, joys, and hope for the future. Yes, life was challenging, but we found creative ways to get away, often to the vacation properties that we couldn't rent or sell. We worked on our relationship so we wouldn't end up blaming each other for our circumstances. It really wasn't anyone's fault. Focusing On The Good Stuff, as Mike Robbins so aptly titled his book, is what helped me and my husband through this difficult period.

I would like to invite you to do the same. Hold on to your life-long dreams and don't bail out because you have had some financial setbacks. Get into the habit of practicing the following suggestions and you will feel more hope and begin to build more positive reserves for yourself now and in your future.

- Make a list of all of the things you are grateful for and why. You will begin to experience a positive internal shift.
- Spend time with positive people who know how to make lemonade out of lemons and have the resilience to bounce back over time. They will encourage you when times are tough.
- Continue to make plans for your future no matter whether you are planning for retirement or are already retired. Planning activities without the big dollar signs can be just as fulfilling.
- Focus on the good aspects of your retirement and the gifts you have been given. Spend time developing your gifts (learn to play an instrument, study a language, develop your physical fitness, improve your bridge game, volunteer, take a class).
- Have fun, laugh, pray daily, and appreciate the good qualities in yourself and others in order to keep your positive energy moving.

A simple aspect of human nature is that we are all too hard on ourselves. In my coaching practice, I have helped many people find more gratitude in their lives because it is often hidden in places they cannot see themselves.

Introspection

The retirement life transition should be a time for introspection and self-reflection. It is a time when we reflect on how we have lived the first part of our lives and what we want to create in the second half of our lives. Looking at who you are, knowing your values, and defining your priorities are all important steps in this stage of life. It is helpful to do your own personal assessment by asking yourself the questions in the Dig Deeper section that follows.

Dig Deeper

What is your attitude toward retirement?

Are you spending time doing the things you love to do?

Do you know what those things are?

Are you reaching out to people who are important in your life and making time for them?

Are you taking good care of yourself?

How will your actions affect the legacy you leave?

What are you grateful for?

What positive people would you like to spend more time with?

What activities do you enjoy that cost very little?

What gifts and talents would you like to develop in your retirement years?

Retirement Resources

Books

<u>Focusing On The Good Stuff: The Power Of Appreciation</u> by Mike Robbins and Richard Carlson

<u>The Power Of Positive Thinking</u> by Norman Vincent Peale

<u>The Third Age: Six Principles Of Growth And Rejuvenation After Forty</u> by William Sadler

<u>Creating Your Best Life: The Ultimate Life List Guide</u> by C. A. Miller and M. B. Fisch

Chapter 8

Redefine Retirement

"This is not your parent's retirement."

Dee Cascio

The New Lifestyle Retirement

We were originally labeled the baby boomers, now we're called elder boomers or even the Age Wave. Regardless of what we are called, our generation is entering the retirement years with a vision and vitality much different than those generations that have preceded us.

AARP's survey of boomers who turned sixty-five in 2011 finds this first wave of the boomer generation generally satisfied with their lives and optimistic about the next third of life. We are envisioning these years as an adventurous and exciting time. In fact, many people now optimistically describe the New Retirement as the Third Quarter, or the Third Age.

Whatever name we use to describe this transitional stage of life, it has become a subject that is receiving more and more attention. When most people hear the word *retirement*, their first fear is outliving their money. Clearly this is an important factor because if you don't have enough money to purchase a plane ticket, you're not going to go anywhere. However, I would argue that it is equally important that you get on the plane that is taking you to someplace you really want to go. Otherwise you might find yourself in Timbuktu.

The second most common issue associated with retirement is where to live in one's retirement years. This is influenced by a number of factors in addition

to income, such as family responsibilities, friendships, special interests, and medical requirements.

However, there are many other lifestyle choices that need to be considered in pre-retirement planning. The sad truth is many of these choices are often overlooked. By taking a more holistic approach, you will be more prepared as you move toward this very important stage in life. These considerations are all the more significant, given that you have the gift of longevity after you retire. Individuals and couples who carefully address all the aspects of retirement during their planning sessions report having a more successful transition experience.

As I've touched on in previous chapters, some of the more important areas that need to be explored in pre-retirement planning are:

- Finances: you and your partner's relationship to money as well as the professional resources for financial planning you have developed over the years. The standard of life created by one's socioeconomic means will affect lifestyle issues like where retirees choose to live, whether or not they will work, and the kind of activities they will pursue
- Work: retirement as it relates to full-time or part-time work, entrepreneurial pursuits, and volunteer activities
- Relationships: the quality and uniqueness of relationships between family members and close friends. Couples and singles should evaluate how those relationships effect one's retirement. Also included are your intimate relationships and the closeness, connection, and emotional bond that will support a couple during the transition to retirement
- Personal growth: the purposeful personal development of an individual's strengths, goals, life-satisfaction and purpose in life
- Leisure: exploring new activities or continuing current activities that create relaxation, pleasure, and a healthy

attitude towards life that include social interaction and solitary relaxation
- Self-care: the extent that you are taking care of your physical and emotional health

Carol's Story—A Successful Retirement

I have a friend and colleague whom I will call Carol. Carol was happily married and all of her children were grown. She and her husband were very excited about their future plans when they retired. He had planned to fully retire and she planned to phase out of her therapy practice over the following year. Six months after her husband retired, he was diagnosed with cancer and died very shortly thereafter. Carol was devastated by the loss of her husband and her life was suddenly turned upside down.

Carol and her husband, who was a physician, were financially set for their retirement. As a result, Carol really didn't need to work but decided to continue her psychotherapy practice at a more relaxed pace. With the extra time Carol had available, she began spending more time visiting her children and grandchildren along with trying new activities.

Although she had been a runner for years, Carol became more active at her health club, took up tap dancing and got into yoga. Being an avid biker, she continued to have fun on biking trips with groups to Europe. She also developed new relationships. As you can see, Carol was able to keep a part of her professional life while enhancing time with her family, traveling, staying engaged with life and the activities that she enjoyed.

Carol now has a successful semi-retirement lifestyle and is very happy. She continues to reduce her work hours and uses the extra time to enjoy all of those activities that are important to her. She also shared that her dad, who remained very active and involved in his retirement, was a wonderful role model for her semi-retirement lifestyle.

Carol's story is a good example of how she integrated all the important areas of her life into her retirement plan. She has continued to work part-time, is socially active, stays intellectually stimulated, uses her creative talents, continues her physical pursuits, enjoys her family, and relaxes alone.

Life Stage Perspectives

Because we all have these bonus years after we leave full-time employment, it's extremely important to do lifestyle planning. Several years ago, I interviewed a number of CPAs and financial planners. I was curious to know what they were hearing from their clients as they were preparing to retire. The concerns that came up most often when they met with clients who were getting closer to retirement were:

- Anxiety about having enough money
- Worry about what they would do to keep busy
- Concerns about their health
- Feared reaction to the loss of social contact with peers
- Uncertainty about where they would live

- Concerns about when one spouse is ready to retire and the other is not and how this would affect their lifestyle planning
- Worry, especially on the part of men, about losing social status associated with their work

Some people say they have so many things they want to do that they will always be very busy. Others plan to just see what happens. Either one of these approaches will work for a while. However, the more important question is "Will you be happy just staying busy or will you need more?" Playing golf, caring for grandchildren, and going out to dinner with friends can be extremely seductive but many report that after about a year, they become restless, bored, unfulfilled, and have a tendency towards complacency and depression. By the time this situation occurs, many don't have enough energy to easily evolve out of this state of being. Once someone becomes depressed, it can be extremely difficult to find the energy to correct the problem. Anti-depressants will help, but the basic problem will still be present. How can you feel better about what you do with the rest of the productive years of your life?

Erik Erickson, the well-known psychoanalyst, defined one of the eight stages of psychosocial development as the stage of *generativity versus stagnation*. This stage represents the years of twenty-five to sixty-five. In this stage of middle adulthood, people settle down, get married, and pursue their careers. Giving back, being productive in one's community, and raising children are all normal tasks in this phase. This stage of development is well defined.

However, if some or all of these tasks are not accomplished, one can become stagnant. It is clear that Erickson saw this stage lasting into the mid-sixties many years ago when he developed his theory.

Erickson named the next life stage *integrity versus despair*, which generally represents ages sixty-five and over. In this stage, as we grow older, we tend to slow down our productivity and explore life as a retired person but we do not stop our productivity. We have a more philosophical approach to reflecting on our lives and our accomplishments. We experience integrity if we see that our lives are successful and meaningful. The dictionary defines *integrity* as "the condition of being whole and complete." This is the time to make sure we have lived our best life and to fill in the blanks if we still have things we want to do.

If we feel guilty about our past or feel that we have not accomplished all of our goals, we might slip into what Erickson called "despair." Despair can lead to depression, a major mental health problem among people in their later years. It is important for us to recognize that this is a time to explore more of who we are, not what we do. That was my awakening.

This is a powerfully exciting stage of life because it is uncharted territory. There is no right or wrong way to do this. Redefining retirement gives our generation a chance to come up with a new definition that is customized to our unique skills and abilities.

Old Versus New Retirement

Years ago I asked my father how he felt about his retirement and he said that he was happy with it. I asked him if he had planned what he was going to do in his retirement and he said that he didn't plan anything because when you are retired "you don't do anything. You let everyone else do the work." I know that he was trying to be funny, but that was my dad's mind-set and that of many in his generation. They did not plan to live very long so retirement meant not doing much. Even though my dad was highly educated, he used very few of his talents after his retirement. I wonder how much this might have contributed to his dementia. As I mentioned earlier, my dad lived until almost ninety-six years old and comes from a family with longevity. Most of his siblings lived into their early nineties. However, his mother and oldest sister both lived to be 103.

It is not only our parents' generation that had this attitude about retirement planning. They also modeled this attitude for their children to emulate. My older brother was an airline pilot with USAir for thirty-three years. Although he knew he faced mandatory retirement when he turned sixty years old, he made no plans before his retirement date. When his initial efforts to find an outlet for his energy and creativity didn't work out, he became bored, frustrated, confused, and depressed. Fortunately, he was eventually able to find a job flying small commercial aircraft for several private companies. This made him happier and more fulfilled while he adds other activities to his retirement lifestyle.

Leisure In Retirement

Undoubtedly, you have worked hard for most of your adult life. During this time, you often sacrificed time for yourself so that you could get a good education, marry, provide for your family, and progress in your career. As you look towards the next stage of your life, you dream about having more time for yourself to do the things that you never had time to do in previous decades. You find yourself fantasizing about traveling, hobbies, physical activities, sports, intellectual pursuits, etc. After you retire from your job or career, you're sure you will settle into a life of leisure with no schedule, no *shoulds,* no *oughts*, and no deadlines. Finally, you believe you will be free. Many current and recent retirees have embraced this old model of retirement from generations that have preceded them. Often, there seems to be a conflict between wanting to be idle and relaxed and staying engaged with some degree of purpose. How do you find a healthy balance between these two conflicting objectives?

Leisure Defined

The dictionary defines *leisure* as the *"freedom or opportunity to do something different; an opportunity afforded by unoccupied time; the state of having time at one's own disposal."* In other words, leisure is the extent to which you have found satisfying activities that allow you to take a break from your work life, leaving you rejuvenated intellectually, emotionally, socially and physically. This is a concept of engagement and not the disengagement attitude of previous generations. All of us deserve to be engaged in activities and interests that reflect who we really are. Bill Sadler, PhD. and James Krefft, PhD., authors of the book entitled Changing Course, found in the research for their book that the Greeks defined leisure as an opportunity for developing a full life with more freedom and reduction of necessity. When one reflects on these various definitions, it is no wonder that retirement and leisure have been so closely linked at the exclusion of many other important aspects of this life stage. Taking a balanced approach, it is important to remember that one person's play is another's work. Because we are all different, we will each define leisure in our own way. Without our own personal definition, we will be missing out on one of life's opportunities to explore our many, less-obvious gifts.

Vacation Versus Leisure

All of us have been on vacation many times throughout our lives. We have discovered that a vacation is a great way to "vacate" the busy, stressful activities of daily living and relax while enjoying the time away with friends and family. As we experience this bliss, we think this is the way retirement should and will be. Because our current life is so complex and busy, we romanticize that in retirement we could easily do this on a daily basis. This is no different than a kid thinking that the ideal job is working in a candy store. After a couple weeks, it's just another job. Unfortunately, the reality is that after retiring, many could find themselves entrapped in a leisurely lifestyle that is not working for them and they do not know why. They have retired to leisure.

Recently, my husband and I were in Tampa at our condo and I was leisurely sitting on the balcony enjoying the view and the warmth of the setting sun. In spite of my knowledge and training, I began to think the very same thoughts. "Wow, relaxing like this would be great full-time with no pressures and stresses. I could do this forever." I realized that it is very natural to think these thoughts as long as you can come back to the reality that anything you do all of the time can be like work and lose its appeal. As I thought about the implications of such a lifestyle, I quickly came back to the reality that this lifestyle would not work for me on a regular basis. In my private practice, I have seen many people retire without a balanced plan to fulfill all their needs. This has led to marital conflict, depression, and a lack of purpose in their lives.

What Is A Leisurely Retirement?

One of the attractions of coaching for me was that it not only reflected the values in my life's work as a psychotherapist but it could help me create a life with more time and space as I transitioned to a modified retirement lifestyle. As I trained for my life/retirement coach certifications, it was apparent to me that defining the best lifestyle for me would require more attention than I had given it in the past.

I had put so much of my identity, time, and energy into my career that there was little time to explore more leisure pursuits. However, since I began to diversify my life by adding a variety of leisure activities along with new learning for my encore career, I am happier, more fulfilled, and more relaxed than I have ever been. A leisurely retirement is experienced when you successfully integrate meaningful life pursuits that give your life purpose and balance. You need a certain degree of variety in your leisure activities as well as personal growth to bring enjoyment and satisfaction to your life.

The challenge for you is to discover what kind of leisure would work best in your life. Without a career to define your identity, how will you discover who you really are? We can still work, but we must do it in a way that creates the freedom to discover other interests and areas of self-exploration.

Ideas To Consider

Here are some thoughts to consider in defining leisure for you.

- No matter what stage of life you are in, be sure to integrate leisure into your life so that you can carry those activities into retirement.
- Be aware that stress can be created by under-loading your lifestyle as well as overloading it.
- Any leisure activity that becomes a full-time endeavor is no longer leisure but has taken the place of a job.

- Leisure provides the gift of serenity, creativity, exercise, intellectual stimulation and rejuvenation, and the opportunity for discovering your authentic self.
- Remember that leisure is only one aspect of retirement. There are many more aspects that need to be integrated into your lifestyle.

Passive Leisure Versus Active Leisure

You may experience and enjoy passive activities like watching television, going to the movies, floating on a boat in the middle of a lake, and watching sports. These kinds of activities are essential when life is busy with the ongoing stresses of work and family responsibilities. However, as we transition to retirement, it is important to avoid the trap of thinking these kinds of passive activities will give you purpose. This is because passivity tends to feed on itself so that the more a person pursues passive activities, the more passive they will become.

In retirement, activities that require creativity, action, and initiative are the kinds of pursuits that will ultimately satisfy the need for staying engaged physically, mentally, and socially. In Ernie Zelinski's book How to Retire Happy, Wild, and Free, he referenced a group of psychologists who separated happiness into two types: feel-good happiness and value-based happiness. They discovered that the feel-good happiness of passive activities eventually led to a decrease in life satisfaction. However, value-based happiness comes from purposeful activities that give us a sense of satisfaction. These activities tap into a deeper sense of who we are and reflect our own personal values.

Easy Leisure Versus Challenging Leisure

There are two other aspects of leisure that are sometimes not as apparent but are still very important. Leisure activities that are passive or very familiar tend to be done with little effort or thought. They are automatic and routine because we have done them over and over again. These include activities such as walking, playing tennis, playing video games, etc. Since my early twenties, I have been an avid runner and walker, enjoying the benefits of exercise and the great outdoors. However, it is all so automatic that I frequently listen to different kinds of music as well as educational tapes to make my walks more interesting and to introduce more intellectual growth.

There is nothing wrong with occasional mindless activities, especially if we are still working. Even if we have retired to another career, these activities, in moderation, can have a beneficial place in our lives.

In retirement, however, leisure needs to satisfy some of the functions that work previously provided: a schedule, socialization, time management, and a sense of accomplishment and purpose. I was surprised to read in Ernie Zelinski's book that there is actually a group called The Academy of Leisure Sciences where scientists study leisure time use. Scientists have found in their research that people get the most satisfaction from leisure activities that are characterized as being harder, more challenging, and that require more sophisticated levels of physical and intellectual energy.

A Healthy Balance Of Various Activities

Regardless of where you are in your life, you should discover the three Es of leisure: explore, experience, and enjoy. Explore, experience, and enjoy all of the leisure choices that are out there and available to you. There are literally hundreds of them including hobbies, sports, college adult courses, volunteer groups, creative pursuits, art, music, dance, and travel. We are never too old to integrate the three Es into our lives. If you haven't taken full advantage of the three Es in your life, make sure you do so in your retirement.

Some of the categories of leisure activities can be found in situations that give you the opportunity to experience social engagement, creativity, life-long learning, physical exercise, hobbies and spending time in solo activities. Remember to focus on what you can do instead of what you can't do.

Begin now to explore this unique opportunity to discover which leisure activities will give you a break from the work that you do. Check out the resources at the end of this chapter to get started.

Dig Deeper

How do you define leisure for yourself?

What leisure activities do you already enjoy?

What activities do you share with others?

How can you create more balance between passive and active leisure activities?

What leisure activity could turn into a work/career/volunteer opportunity for you?

What do you still hope to:

- Explore?

- Experience?

- Enjoy?

Retirement Resources

Books

<u>Changing Course: Navigating Life After Fifty</u> by William Sadler and James Krefft

<u>How To Retire Happy, Wild, And Free: Retirement Wisdom That You Won't Get From Your Financial Advisor</u> by Ernie Zelinski

Web Sites

101 hobby ideas

http://www.findmeahobby.com

New places to explore

http://www.iexplore.com

Psychological Assessment Resources' Leisure Activities Finder (LAF), a booklet of over 700 activities that match the personality finder, the Holland Code

http://www.parinc.com

Chapter 9

Reinvent Yourself And Your Career

"Don't simply retire from something: have something to retire to."

Harry Emerson Fosdick

Career Orientation For Retirees

I am always interested in hearing stories about people's ideas for life planning. I was talking to a friend who said her father, a sixty-two year-old electrical engineer, was planning to retire in about a year. Apparently, his retirement plan consists of moving to Florida because that is where his best friend lives. However, he has absolutely no idea what he will do once he is there. His daughter commented, "He won't last more than six months before he is back to work." She was quite concerned about how he would handle this important transition.

My friend's story about her dad's plan reminded me of when my father retired. He began his career as a teacher in a one-room school in upstate New York. My father had worked his way from teaching in a one-room school to becoming a principal of the largest elementary school in the city of Elmira, where we grew up. One day he was a very successful full-time administrator of a school and the next day, he had nothing to do except play golf, travel once or twice a year, and do handy-man projects around the house. It is important to note that money was not an issue for my father because he planned well for his retirement. I remember him spending hours reviewing the performance of his stocks, selling and buying to meet his goals. However, while he had spent decades working on his financial plan, he had never given any thought as to how he would actually spend his time in retirement. If he had spent 10% less time on financial aspects of his retirement and used that time for lifestyle planning, the outcome might have been different. Thirty-five years later, I regret that he didn't make better use of his life experience, education, and wisdom. His skills and experience would have been so valuable to many, young and old, if he had only recareered or volunteered.

My dad is not an isolated example. As the Boomer generation leaves traditional work daily, how will they repurpose their skills and talent? Conversely, how will employers compensate for this incredible loss of skilled, professional talent and intellectual capital disappearing on a daily basis? What policy changes will our nation's employers have to make in order to entice their older workers to stay and mentor younger workers?

Planning for this important stage of life, which is part of everyone's developmental process, can be daunting. It can also be the beginning of creating more exciting choices for all of us. It really depends on your attitude and approach to this life transition. There are so many possibilities that can define a dream retirement consisting of work, leisure, volunteerism, travel, education, hobbies, etc. Most of us have worked for a very long time and may need support and direction to realize the choices that are available to us. In fact, there are so many options that many people are simply overwhelmed by all of the possibilities.

So Many Choices

My husband likes to tell the story about the first new house he purchased in the mid-1960s. As part of the purchase, he was instructed to come by the sales office one afternoon so he could pick out the carpets for the house. They presented him with one carpet grade that was available in five or six basic colors. He said he made his selection in several moments and was on his way.

Fast forward seven years and he was ready to make a second new house purchase. Once again, the salesperson requested that he come by to select the carpets for the house. When he arrived there was a bewildering selection of possibilities. There was nylon, wool, and any number of synthetic fiber combinations. There was also sculptured, shag, plush, short nap, and a variety of other styles of carpeting. Finally, they brought out books showing every color in the rainbow for each type of carpet selection. Although he prides himself on being a very decisive individual, he said he was totally overwhelmed. He had to make an appointment for the following day to finish his selection.

Going into retirement is a lot like my husband's story of carpet selection. Subject only to financial considerations, your health, and your spouse's concurrence, you can do virtually anything you want to do. The possibilities are endless and therein lies the dilemma. There are so many options and possibilities that it's difficult for some of us to make a decision. For many, this is where the paralysis begins to set in. This is such a common occurrence that there's actually an expression for it: *Analysis Paralysis*. I believe this is why so many people continue to work even though they could retire. Since they can't decide what they want to do, it is just easier to keep doing the same thing they have been doing for years.

Have you considered how you would like to spend your time once you retire? With the focus on who you are as opposed to what you have done in your career, this stage requires a letting go of who you were in your past career in order to move on to a more holistic definition of who you are without work defining you. This mindset is filled with all kinds of opportunities.

Work provides a number of important elements in our lives that we must find ways to replace in our retirement careers. One way or another, you have to replace these elements or you will end up feeling bored and dissatisfied. Staying "busy" won't be enough.

An easy acronym to help you remember these job attributes that you need to replace is WORK PROVIDES:

Transition Strategies
for Life & Work

To have a successful retirement, it's essential to replace many of the benefits that your current employment provides. The acronym below will help remind you of what

WORK PROVIDES

W	WAGES	Income, savings & benefits (vacations, holidays, sick leave)
O	ORDER	Organization, structure, routine, harmony
R	RELATIONSHIPS	Colleagues, associates, clients, friends, coworkers, etc.
K	KNOWLEDGE	New products, education, on-the-job training

P	PURPOSE	Reason to get up, meaning, something to look forward to
R	RECOGNITION	Acknowledgment, title, respect, appreciation, admiration
O	OPPORTUNITY	Promotions, new work, new acquaintances, new ideas
V	VALUE	Providing quality products or services, meaning of work
I	IDENTITY	Embracing company's goals, position, being part of a team
D	DIRECTION	Goals, knowing what needs to be done and by when
E	EXPERIENCE	Time and place to achieve and develop skills
S	STABILITY	Predictability, consistency, permanence, strength

©2014 Dee Cascio, LPC, LMFT, BCC
www.lifeandworktransitions.com
Dee@lifeandworktransitions.com

W – Wages
Income, savings and benefits (vacations, holidays, sick leave)

O – Order
Organization, structure, routine, harmony

R – Relationships
Colleagues, associates, clients, friends, coworkers

K – Knowledge
New products, education, on-the-job training

P – Purpose
Reason to get up, meaning, something to look forward to

R – Recognition
Acknowledgment, title, respect, appreciation, admiration

O – Opportunity
Promotions, new work, new acquaintances, new ideas

V– Value
Producing quality products or services, meaning of work

I – Identity
Embracing company's goals, position, being part of a team

D – Direction
Goals, knowing what needs to be done and by when

E – Experience
Time and place to achieve and develop skills

S – Stability
Predictability, consistency, permanence, strength

These requirements can be satisfied in various ways such as:

- Full-time work in the same or different field. Remember that the impending employee shortage should give you greater leverage to design your ideal work situation.
- Part-time work in the same or different field in the form of job sharing or other variations.
- Volunteering in a variety of fields that could turn into a job or a new career path.
- Entrepreneurial pursuits
- A combination of part-time work and volunteering.

The question remains: what will fulfill you? What factors will determine how the elements that WORK PROVIDES, listed above, will be satisfied in your life and create balance and harmony? Even leisure activities, life-long learning, and hobbies can provide some of what work used to provide.

Please take some time to explore the Web sites listed at the end of this chapter. They contain valuable resources that will guide and empower you in making important decisions and will optimize the possibility of a successful retirement.

Staying Engaged In Retirement

Recently, I was working with a client who was preparing to retire within the next year. As we discussed her plans, she shared some of her concerns about this upcoming transition. One of her biggest fears was that without the social stimulation of her work environment, she might become detached and disengaged from life. Many of her friends were colleagues at work. She had visions of being alone too much and not leaving her house for long periods of time. She was anxious about this because she watched another family member retire and gradually begin living a reclusive lifestyle. I was impressed that she realized that "disengaging" was a significant reason that could contribute to an unhappy or unsuccessful retirement. Many people fail to understand the importance of the structured, ready-made social environment work provides for them until they lose it.

The Challenges Of Staying Engaged

The landscape of life as you have always known it will change after you leave work. You will be faced with the challenges of how you will adapt to those changes. I have discovered in my private practice that one of the biggest changes that my clients experience in retirement will be losing the social benefits they have enjoyed from their work environment. Every day, they woke up knowing they would commute to work, perform certain requirements of their jobs, and socialize as well as engage in personal conversations with friends, co-workers, and perhaps clients as well. After eight to ten hours, they would return home to spend the rest of the day with their families.

This pattern, repeated daily for thirty to forty years, creates a dilemma. What will happen when work as a vehicle for socialization, as well as the predictable routine of activities, changes? How will you stay engaged, satisfied, and purposeful in your life? You have to recognize that you may need more social interaction than others. How will you meet this need regardless of how much or little you think you need it? All aspects of life are constantly changing but it is how you navigate these changes that will determine how successful your retirement will be.

In Changing Course, by Sadler and Krefft, they summarize a prestigious MacArthur study that followed people who were living vital, healthy, and active lives into their seventies and beyond. After examining the lifestyles of these successful agers, they determined that the choices one makes, rather than heredity, determine health, vitality, and improved quality of life. This study also stressed the importance of social engagement, a strong network of social support, and continued life-long learning to sustain a high level of personal, social, and cognitive functioning. As I read about the authors of this study, I was pleased to see one of the authors who pioneered this study was an eighty-year-old psychologist.

Abraham Maslow, a renowned psychologist, developed his hierarchy of needs that are essential to life and one of them was belonging: the need to be a part of a group. If your group is only your spouse, you may experience some relational conflict because your spouse can't possibly meet all of your social needs.

When I first started my private therapy practice, I shared my office condo with five other therapists who each had their own office. Much of my day-to-day social network was built into that work environment. A few years ago, anticipating my own gradual easing into retirement, I decided to downsize my office and buy a smaller office condo. Because of this change, I no longer had colleagues sharing my office space and providing the daily social interaction I had known for years.

I knew being in a solo practice with no colleagues in my office would require me to intentionally create ways to interact with people outside of my office. As a result, I made plans to go to lunches and professional meetings. Even though I belong to several professional groups, I decided to join the Herndon Rotary Club, when invited, so I could stay engaged and meet people from different walks of life. This was the best decision I could have made for my future. It has given me the opportunity to become a part of an organization that does good work in the community and all over the world. It also gives me a volunteer organization that I can continue to be a part of for the rest of my life if I choose.

Ways To Stay Engaged

How will you stay engaged and socially vibrant after you leave the work environment? There are many ways to stay active in retirement if you have a positive attitude, are resourceful, and have a good support system. Here are some suggestions for ways to stay engaged and connected in retirement.

1. Volunteer your skills and talents in your community

2. Take a class at a local college or at the many Oshi Life Long Learning Institutes associated with many colleges and universities

3. Explore possible part-time job opportunities doing something challenging and fun

4. Join a local civic organization

5. Plan a weekly or monthly lunch with friends and colleagues to nurture already established friendships

6. Take an art class

7. Spend a day with your grandchildren doing fun things

8. Pursue a hobby in a bigger way

9. Join or start a book club

10. Find ways of making people in your life feel important

Planning now for how you will stay engaged will help your retirement transition go much more smoothly.

Pursuing Meaningful Work In Retirement

For most of history, the meaning of life and work were based on survival. We needed to work to live. When inexpensive energy and industrialization increased productivity, some speculated that we would use the extra time we gained for more relaxation. The reality is that we began using this extra time to work longer and harder, especially those of us in the post-war boomer generation who value the work ethic and high- achieving lifestyle. Yet for many boomers, work they would consider "meaningful" remains elusive. It is often difficult for them to pinpoint what is missing or what it is that would give their work lives more meaning.

Discover Your Genius

Ultimately, it is not about the work we do or have done. It is about whether or not our work is aligned with what Dick Richards calls "your genius." In his book <u>Is Your Genius At Work?</u>, he uses this term to identify the unique intersection between what you are good at (your gift) and what you love to do (your passion). Once you have identified your unique gift and passion, the challenge is to find that elusive intersection between your gift and an "unmet need" in the world so that you can make a living at it. Once you have found this intersection of gift and passion, you will be able to confidently move toward creating opportunities that meet that need. *If you can get your gift and passion in alignment with a need, suddenly work becomes more like play, especially in retirement.* This is genius. Many boomers, without even realizing it, are re-careering using this mindset.

What Gets You Up In The Morning?

What is the definition of meaningful work? You might want to try doing an attitude check when the alarm goes off in the morning. If the alarm rings and you are eager to get out of bed because you are excited by what you're doing and each new day is certain to provide some worthy experience then the chances are pretty good that you have identified your passion—regardless of the notoriety you experience at work.

If on the other hand you're not eager to face the day most of the time, you might want to consider another career or job within your career area. These days, more and more people in that situation are turning toward self-employment opportunities as the key to matching up purpose with genius. All the challenges of figuring out what will bring meaning to your life and how to integrate this into career possibilities come along with that transition.

Feeling Fulfilled In The Retirement Of Your Choice

These days 62% of boomers between the ages of sixty-five and sixty-nine are working full-time or plan to work at least part-time in their retirement. Who would have thought that we would be using *work* and *retirement* in the same breath and sentence? However, today it is common to hear people talk about including work in their retirement plans. At this life stage, it is almost a requirement that you know and understand your relationship to meaningful work or you will not be satisfied with your retirement lifestyle.

What Will Your Story Be?

To get a better understanding of your relationship with meaningful work, Mark Guterman, co-founder of MeaningfulCareers.com, suggests imagining a future situation in which you will be telling others your story of how work and meaning finally came together for you. To prepare the story, he suggests reflecting on questions such as the following:

- How is your soul enriched and enlivened through your work?

- How does your work contribute to the future?

- How does your sense of "who you are" show up in your work?

- For whom do you work?

- How has your relationship with work changed over the course of your life?

- What role has serendipity, coincidence, luck, etc. played in your work life?

- How have fun, play, and humor been a part of meaningful work?

- Do you have a philosophy, mission, vision, or goal that guides your work life? If so, what is it and how did you come to it?

- What poetry, quotes, sayings, prayers, music, spiritual writings, pictures, photographs, paintings, etc. represent and/or guide your work life? How do they impact your work?

All of these questions are good coaching questions to get you thinking about how work fits into your retirement lifestyle. Determine whether or not you have work in its proper perspective before you leave your job permanently or transition to another career. Be sure about the reasons you are working. And remember, work *and* play are equally important for a balanced life.

Discovering Your Unique Purpose In Retirement

Many in our hard-working generation are looking forward to the day they retire. The expectation is that many of us will just go with the flow, relax, and do the things we always wanted to do. However, it doesn't take long before one day resembles the next and you are developing habits that don't serve you well. Sometimes these bad habits are so subtle that the damage they cause happens before you even know it. Eventually you might realize that because you have always been part of a high-achieving generation, you will need much more purpose in life than you will get in a traditional retirement. When we were working and raising families, our life purpose was built-in. We knew what was expected of us and what we expected of ourselves. However, we now have fewer obligations to others, so we have to create a life based on our own personal interests, values, skills, and passions. However, this flexibility and freedom may be impacted if you have the responsibility of aging parents or children still at home.

How will you spend your time? What will give you the sense of purpose that has been built into every other stage of your life? Along with fewer obligations there is also less information readily available about what we call the introspective shift that will occur in your life at this critical stage. There are no two people alike, so this transition requires a different kind of preparation that is not concrete or well understood.

What Gives Your Life Meaning?

There are numerous ways you can create a foundation of self-trust and open communication between you and your partner. Being honest is necessary to help you to move forward with more self-assurance. You should recognize this will be the first time in your adult life that you will be your own boss. For the first time since you were young, obligations to others are a backdrop and you can put you and your partner first. This realization begins with how you want to _be_ in your life. While we might sometimes mourn the loss, it is a blessing that more and more of your work obligations and family responsibilities have come to a resting place. This transition will take on more importance and urgency as you no longer have a multitude of external factors driving your every decision on a daily basis.

The longings, ideas, questions, and concerns regarding this movement towards retirement occur at several levels: _internally,_ which includes the feelings and thoughts about this stage, and _externally_ through planning and taking action. In all of my training, I have learned that doing what you love is the cornerstone of a successful life. For example, for me personally, it is clear that teaching, counseling, and life coaching are what I love to do. It reflects my values and skills, gives me purpose, and brings me joy. It requires that I continue to learn, grow, and challenge myself. These are important objectives I know must be a part of my personal retirement plan. So ask yourself: what is it that you love to do? What will get you up in the morning when you no longer have to be at the office by 8:00 AM?

Living On Purpose

When you are living on purpose, you are consciously in touch with your talents, skills, gifts, strengths, and values. Living on purpose requires time for introspection, thoughtful reflection about your life, and the ability to move forward using this knowledge. Once you are aware of these aspects of yourself, you are then ready to move into the decision-making process about where these parts of yourself can best be expressed. Is there a cultural problem, cause, new career, etc. that is calling you to exercise all of those countless gifts you possess? In Repacking Your Bags, R. Leider and D. Shapiro said it well. "Purpose is not a goal. A goal is something that can be reached. A purpose is never achieved. It exits before you and lives on after you are gone."

Finding Your Purpose

Having a purpose in life will give your life meaning no matter what life stage you are in. While personally doing this exploration, I found life purpose in using my gifts of listening, empathy, compassion, resourcefulness, and creativity. Throughout my career, these gifts have allowed me to help people grow through self-understanding and move forward to live healthier and more satisfying lives filled with purpose and meaning. Do you know what your purpose is? Take time to reflect on the following questions:

1. Sit quietly and reflect on your talents, strengths, and skills. Write them down. Ask those you love and trust to reflect on what they experience with you and give you feedback about your gifts.
2. What issues, social challenges, or causes in your environment, your life, or the world stir passion and interest where you can use your gifts and talents discovered in #1?
3. Can you develop a plan that will be focused on implementing action towards this purpose?
4. What kind of support do you need to move forward?
5. How will you know that you are on the right journey for you?

Dig Deeper

What fulfills you?

What gives your life purpose?

What are your unique gifts?

What are you passionate about?

Where do purpose, giftedness, and passion come together in your life?

How will you stay engaged in your retirement years?

How will you replace the benefits of work?

What are the pros and cons for you regarding these after-retirement options:

- Full-time work

- Part-time work

- Volunteering

- Becoming an entrepreneur

- A combination of these

Retirement Resources

Books

Changing Course: Navigating Life After Fifty by William Sadler and James Krefft

Is Your Genius At Work? 4 Key Questions To Ask Before Your Next Career Move by Dick Richards

Repacking Your Bags: Lighten Your Load For The Rest Of Your Life by Richard Leider and David Shapiro

Web Sites

Career assessment tests

http://www.hollandcodes.com

Careers at AARP

http://www.aarp.org/careers

Encore careers

http://www.civicventures.org

Find a great place to volunteer

http://www.volunteermatch.org

Guiding you to meaningful work

http://www.meaningfulcareers.com

Job network

http://www.monster.com

Opportunities to change the world

http://www.handsonnetwork.org

Starting your own business

http://www.entrepreneur.com

The Wall Street Journal's online business section

http://www.startupjournal.com

Tools to help job seekers

http://www.careeronestop.org

Chapter 10

Leave A Legacy

"Life isn't a matter of milestones, but of moments."

Rose Kennedy

What Is A Legacy?

A legacy is something that is left behind by the preceding generation. It can be either positive or negative, and each person's legacy is unique. It's up to you to determine your purpose and your contribution.

A legacy can also be something of ourselves left behind, or it can be a meaningful object that is passed down from one generation to the next. Legacies don't have to be physical objects—they can also be ideas, values, attitudes, and traditions. For example, a family might pass a business from one generation to the next, leaving the legacy of the business and an entrepreneurial spirit along with a strong work ethic, perseverance, and commitment.

Albert Pine may have said it best when he wrote "What we have done for ourselves alone dies with us. What we have done for others and the world remains and is immortal."

My Parents' Legacy

I've often thought about what my parents passed down to me and my siblings. I have reflected on my parents' lives and how hard they worked as first-generation Italian-Americans to create a better life for all of us. My dad received his education through the G. I. Bill after serving in WWII. He completed most of his education while helping to raise five young children. As a teacher, he always worked during the summers at other jobs to meet financial commitments that were difficult to do on a teacher's salary. After he finished his Master's Degree in Education and became a principal, he worked year-round at a better salary. While still working, my dad also contributed to the community by volunteering through the Rotary Club, the American Red Cross, and the American Cancer Society.

My mother went through a three-year registered nursing program at St. Joseph's Hospital in Elmira, New York before she moved to Buffalo to work at an orphanage. Before she and my father married, my mother returned to St. Joseph's Hospital to work as a RN in the OB/GYN department where she received her training. She loved her work, especially caring for the infants. She was very good at supporting new mothers and educating them on how to care for their infants. I remember my mother getting up in the middle of the night to go to the hospital because a friend or family member wanted her support and expertise when their child was born. When someone was sick, she would often go to their homes to help nurse them. My mother was an instructor in the Nurse Training Program towards the end of her career, before she was diagnosed with cancer and died at age fifty-four.

While raising five children on two salaries, my parents were always financially responsible and stretched what they had to feed, clothe, and educate all of us. We socialized with extended family and friends often, especially during the holidays and special occasions. Italian families will find any reason to gather and celebrate. Although it wasn't easy at times and they had their challenges, they made it through because they worked together. We were expected to help in whatever way we could. Our weekly worship together in the church of our faith also gave us a sense of community and instilled good values.

How Their Legacy Has Affected My Life

As a baby boomer, I have reflected back on my life and what my parents' legacy gave me. They passed down the following values and beliefs:

1. It is important to get an education no matter what sacrifices you have to make.

2. Family is very important so never neglect those relationships.

3. As a parent and spouse, do whatever it takes to support your family.

4. Be dependable and reliable so that your loved ones know they can always count on you.

5. Develop a strong work ethic while nurturing the gifts of perseverance, commitment, flexibility, and patience.

6. Integrate the positive values and standards you learned as a child with what you have learned as an adult.

7. Give of yourself to your community as much as possible.

8. Make your career your calling so that it truly reflects who you really are.

9. Through tough economic times, you do what you have to do to survive.

My husband and I added number ten to this list:

10. Enjoy the values and rewards along with the challenges of creating and running your own business as you model a strong work ethic along with following your passion and calling.

Legacy For The Baby Boomer Generation

This list reflects not only my parents' legacy to us but my husband's and my legacy to the next generation within our families. People say this is the worst recession since WWII. Since post-WWII, we boomers have had the opportunity to provide a strong and positive legacy for surviving and thriving. Often struggle builds character and confidence, strengthens bonds, stimulates creativity, and makes us appreciate what we do have. Make the following your *legacy of thriving* in difficult times.

- If you have lost your job, face the disappointment then begin your job search for a new and perhaps better job.

- If you have lost some of your retirement funds, develop a plan that could allow you to continue to work longer but at a different pace and at something you love to do.

- Find ways you can cut back on expenses until things turn around.

- Be responsible about your health and take care of health problems so you can hold on to your independence for as long as possible.

- Maintain a positive attitude towards your life, your spouse, and your future because you know you are truly doing the best you can.

My Challenge To You

Take some time over the next few days to think about what legacies were passed on to you and what you are passing down to your children and future generations. Write them down. Embrace the positive legacies. If you identify some negative legacies, give yourself an opportunity to change those in your lifetime. Leave behind a legacy you can be proud of.

What If You Have Yet To Create A Legacy?

If you don't know what legacy you might leave behind, consider the gift that keeps on giving. Volunteer and give of yourself.

Volunteers, who make a difference every day, are the unsung heroes of our communities and nation. Volunteers have rebuilt neighborhoods, fed the poor, won elections, and clothed the homeless. Have you wanted to help a child learn how to read, wrap gifts for less fortunate families at your local church during the Christmas season, work at a soup kitchen, or collect winter coats for the homeless? Our communities abound with opportunities to give back, but how many of us answer the call?

How Will You Answer The Call To Service?

According to Elizabeth Andrew "Volunteers don't necessarily have the time; they just have the heart."

When we work long hours, week after week, year after year, there is often little energy left to volunteer your skills and time to your favorite cause or charity. Some of us have stretched ourselves pretty thin while working, going to school, and raising a family. After feeling exhausted and depleted, we don't feel like we have much energy left to volunteer. Consequently, many of us do the next easiest thing, which is to donate money, and there's nothing wrong with that.

While I was working hard building my therapy practice, the only volunteering I did was donating blood every several months. I did some casual volunteering here and there, but it wasn't consistent. Instead, I raised money, participated in walks for various causes, and supported my friends and neighbors in their charitable pursuits. That has changed in the last several years as a result of making a more concerted effort to give back. By joining Rotary where there are numerous opportunities to volunteer my time, skills, and energy throughout the year, I have accomplished my goal.

I've heard many pre-retirees and those recently retired say that they've "been there, done that and now I just want to rest." Great! Go ahead and rest for a while. However, you will eventually catch up on your rest, organize your closets, and meet up with friends before you begin to wonder what else there is for you to do with your hard earned bonus years. Retirement, whether it's part-time or full-time, provides the extra time to give of your talents and skills to others less fortunate.

The Boomerang Effect Of Volunteering

"The best way to find yourself is to lose yourself in service to others," said M. K. Gandhi. No matter what stage of life we are in, volunteering has benefits that have been tested and researched by many. Researchers at the University of Michigan studied a group of adult men and found that those who volunteered their time, skills, and money were happier, more positive about their life, and outlived their peers who weren't so altruistic. As we give of ourselves, we often receive more than we give. We find ourselves enjoying a more positive attitude along with greater feelings of satisfaction. Many have reported re-experiencing the same positive feelings by just remembering their volunteer experiences.

Sonya Lyubomirsky, author of The How of Happiness, researcher, and Professor of Psychology at the University of California—Riverside, has found that helping others may build more appreciation for our communities and neighborhoods. Service to others also creates feelings of appreciation and gratitude for what we have when we see those less fortunate than we are. We also have the opportunity to model for our peers as well as our adult children and grandchildren the art of volunteering.

Many who have retired and begun volunteering have found this experience provides some of the same benefits work previously provided. People say they derive meaning and purpose from activities that help others live better lives. Volunteering gives structure to the day and gives people an opportunity to connect socially with other volunteers as well as with those they are helping. Altruism can be very gratifying, and it helps make the world a better place.

By assessing your skills, strengths, interests, and passions, you may find a volunteer organization that is a good fit for you. Decide if you want to volunteer for a large or small organization, how involved you want to be, and how long you want to commit. Volunteering can also help you discover a new career path during your retirement transition. Many have turned volunteering into paid work or created a non-profit business from their volunteer experience.

Where Do You Want To Put Your Energy?

When choosing where, when, and how you want to volunteer, take into consideration the following suggestions:

1. Do what you feel passion about, gives meaning to your life, or can become part of your legacy
2. Explore your current skills and think about learning new skills if necessary
3. Find one volunteer activity you can do with your life partner to make your relationship more interesting as well as create more social contacts
4. Be open to a volunteer activity becoming a paying position if the opportunity arises
5. If you have physical limitations, consider volunteering online by looking at the website: http://www.onlinevolunteering.org.
6. Explore the Web sites on the Resources page to give you more ideas

Remember, giving of yourself to those in need will help you to leave a legacy for future generations.

Dig Deeper

How satisfied are you with the legacy you have created?

If you are not satisfied, what can you do to share

- Your passion
- Whatever gives meaning to your life
- Something that can become part of your legacy

How does your legacy reflect who you are or who you might want to become in this life stage?

What skills could you use as a volunteer right now?

What skills might you develop for future use?

Where might you and your partner volunteer together?

Retirement Resources

Books

The How of Happiness: A New Approach To Getting The Life You Want by Sonja Lyubomirsky

Web Sites

Connecting non-profit boards and new leaders

http://www.boardnetusa.org

Find a great place to volunteer

http://www.volunteermatch.org

Find a volunteer opportunity

http://www.volunteer.gov

Find meaningful work and significant service

www.civicventures.org/nextchapter

Improve K-3 literacy by volunteering as a tutor

http://www.experiencecorps.org

Jobs, organizations, volunteer opportunities, resources

http://www.idealist.org

Operation Hope, the global leader for financial dignity

http://www.operationhope.org

Opportunities to change the world

http://www.handsonnetwork.org

United Nations online volunteer opportunities

http://www.onlinevolunteering.org

Additional Retirement Resources

Books
Don't Retire, Rewire! by Jeri Sedlar and Rick Miners

Finding Meaning In The Second Half Of Life: How To Finally, Really Grow Up by James Hollis

Prime Time: How Baby Boomers Will Revolutionize Retirement And Transform America by Marc Freedman

The Joy Of Not Working: A Book For The Retired, Unemployed And Overworked by Ernie Zelinski

Too Young To Retire: 101 Ways To Start The Rest Of Your Life by Marika and Howard Stone

What's Next? Follow Your Passion And Find Your Dream Job by Kerry Hannon

Web Sites

AARP

http://www.aarp.org

Assess your readiness for retirement coaching

http://www.retirementlifestylestrategies.com/quiz.html

About Dee Cascio, LPC, LMFT, ACC, BCC

Dee wants to help you make the best of your life for the rest of your life. Whether you are experiencing a life or work transition, exploring a career change, assisting aging parents with retirement decisions, or planning for your own future, she has the experience, skills, and resources you need to make these transitions successfully.

Dee is a

- Licensed Professional Counselor
- Licensed Marriage and Family Therapist
- Certified Imago Relationship Therapist
- Certified Life Coach, Coach University
- Certified Retirement Coach, Retirement Options

- Certified ReCareer Coach, Retirement Options
- CCE Board Certified Coach
- Member of the American Association of Marriage and Family Therapists
- Member of the Virginia Association of Counselors
- Member of the International Association of Coaches
- Author of Where Will YOU Retire? A Retirement Guide And Exercises For Deciding Where To Retire, Buy A Second Home, Or Relocate
- Author of the Life And Work Transition Strategies blog and monthly newsletter
- Co-author of Contagious Optimism—Uplifting Lessons of Happiness, Love and Success From Around the Globe
- Sought-after speaker and workshop leader

For online seminars and workshops near you, visit http://www.lifeandworktransitions.com.

Made in the USA
Middletown, DE
09 September 2017